TURKEY IN
POST-SOVIET
CENTRAL ASIA

The Former Soviet South project is sponsored by:

- A. Meredith Jones & Company Ltd
- B.A.T Industries plc
- The British Petroleum Company Ltd
- Ente Nazionale Idrocarburi S.p.A.
- John Laing International plc
- Statoil

Series editor: Edmund Herzig

FORMER SOVIET SOUTH PROJECT

TURKEY IN POST-SOVIET CENTRAL ASIA

Gareth M. Winrow

THE ROYAL INSTITUTE OF
INTERNATIONAL AFFAIRS
Russia and CIS Programme

CONTENTS

SUMMARY

As the Soviet Union unravelled Turkish officials suddenly assumed a great interest in developments in the Central Asian Turkic republics – namely, Kazakhstan, Uzbekistan, Turkmenistan and Kyrgyzstan. In spite of common historical, cultural, linguistic and ethnic links, in practice Turkey had paid little attention to these territories until the final months of Gorbachev's presidency. In a burst of euphoria, promoted in part by the interest of the leaderships of the Turkic republics, and supported by the West – fearful of the possible expansion of Iranian influence – Turkey rapidly became actively involved in Central Asia. Rising nationalist feeling in Turkey also encouraged Turkish officials and the public alike to think in terms of Turkic solidarity and brotherhood. Different sets of policy objectives and ambitions towards Central Asia appeared to emerge among various ministries, political parties, agencies and lobbies.

The disappointment of the poorly prepared first Turkic Summit, convened in October 1992, resulted in lowered expectations on Ankara's part. In addition to cultivating ties with Turkey, the Central Asian leaderships were eager for economic and security reasons to remain on good terms with Moscow and were keen to develop relations with other states interested in the region, such as Iran. However, Turkey has remained a key player in post-Soviet Central Asia. Turkish businessmen and officials in Ankara have expanded their economic interests in the area. Credits have been offered to boost trade turnover and support the extensive activities of Turkish construction workers in Central Asia. In general, Turkish policy towards the Turkic republics has become motivated by both sentiment and self-interest, as shown by developments up to and immediately after the second Turkic Summit, convened in October 1994. Although the priority of the Çiller government is still to develop closer relations with Western Europe, Turkey is likely to remain a major player in Central Asia.

ABOUT THE AUTHOR

Gareth M. Winrow is an Associate Professor in the Department of Political Science and International Relations at Boğaziçi University, Istanbul, Turkey. He is currently involved in a group project sponsored by the US Institute of Peace to study Turkey and the Kurdish issue. His most recent publications include *Where East meets West: Turkey and the Balkans* (London: Institute for European Defence and Strategic Studies, 1993), and articles on Turkish foreign policy, regional security issues in the Caucasus and Central Asia, and problems of European security in general, in journals such as *Central Asian Survey*, the *Oxford International Review*, the *Journal of South Asian and Middle Eastern Studies*, and *European Security*.

ACKNOWLEDGMENTS

I would like to thank all those who offered constructive comments in the study group at Chatham House to discuss the first draft of this paper. I am particularly grateful to Roy Allison and Edmund Herzig for their encouragement and editorial work. The contributions of Peter Roland, Tarık Bayazit and Didem Mersin-Alici have been especially helpful. My thanks also go to those people who were willing to be interviewed. Last but not least, special thanks are due to Nazan and Marc Sinan for their patience, understanding and constant support.

March 1995   Gareth Winrow

1 INTRODUCTION

In his speech at the opening of the Turkish Grand National Assembly in September 1994, President Suleyman Demirel likened Turkey to an opened gate through which Europe and the US could enter and develop relations with the newly independent states of the Transcaucasus and Central Asia. Referring to the need to revive the Silk Route, Demirel explained that in the near future Turkey would become an energy terminal for the oil and gas of Central Asia and the Middle East. The Turkish President emphasized that Turkey was not in competition with any state in the Eurasian region, and noted that Turkey and Russia could work as partners to integrate this region with the rest of the world.[1] Demirel appeared eager to impress upon the West the importance of Turkey as a conduit through which economic ties with post-Soviet Central Asia could be cultivated. He was aware that Turkey could play a significant role in helping to bring the newly independent 'Turkic' states politically and economically into the wider international community, with economic benefits accruing to Turkey at the same time. He also noted that other states, most notably Russia, had interests and concerns in post-Soviet Central Asia. In practice, though, within Turkey there appear to be different sets of policy objectives and ambitions towards the region. Certain groups and individuals in Turkey do not necessarily share the line of the Turkish Ministry of Foreign Affairs.

Quite clearly the end of the Cold War has necessitated a reassessment of policy-making in Ankara, as Turkey is no longer able to depict itself as a key NATO front-line state bordering a hostile Soviet Union. Nevertheless, in line with a policy which may be traced back to Ataturk and indeed even earlier, the current government of Tansu Çiller remains determined to demonstrate Turkey's Western credentials. In addition to membership of NATO, another means of pursuing this policy is by seeking to boost Turkey's prestige and international stature with the aim of securing full admission into the European Union – perceived by many officials in Ankara as the ultimate Western club. In this context, the disintegration of the Soviet Union and the emergence of newly independent Turkic states in the Transcaucasus and Central Asia provided Turkish officials with opportunities and challenges. An active involvement in the region, with

---

1. *Turkish Daily News* (*TDN*), 2 September 1994.

1

the authorities in Ankara eager to promote the attractiveness of the so-called Turkish model of economic and political development, could enhance Turkey's international profile and thereby perhaps improve its prospects of eventual admission into the EU.

One product of the end of the Cold War era has been the unleashing of the destructive forces of extremist nationalism – most obviously observed in Europe with the implosion in former Yugoslavia and the brutal practice of ethnic cleansing. The plight of the Bosnian Muslims has struck a sensitive chord in the hearts and minds of the Turkish population. At the same time, since Turkey is no longer perceived as so important to Western security interests now that the tangible Soviet threat has disappeared, the United States and Western Europe have become increasingly critical of Turkish policy towards its Kurdish people, and cases of human rights violations committed by the Turkish authorities are receiving more publicity. Entry into the EU remains exceedingly unlikely in the foreseeable future on account of the Greek veto, which will not be lifted while the impasse over the Cyprus question continues. Turkey itself is also affected by the rising tide of nationalist feeling. Turkish officials are exasperated at the likelihood of the newly democratizing East European states jumping the queue to join the EU, and are furious at perceived double standards with regard to Western concern for the human rights of the Kurds while the flagrant abuse of codes of civilized behaviour in Bosnia are simultaneously ignored.

The Çiller government, although not abandoning the goal of entry to the EU, has been compelled to toe a more nationalist line in order to prevent outflanking by the nationalist-Islamicist opposition embodied in the Welfare Party and to curry favour with the resurgent right-wing National Action Party led by Alpaslan Türkeş. This nationalist line could lead to a strengthening of anti-Western feeling which could ultimately result in Turkey retreating into a form of semi-isolationism. Disillusionment with the failure of major international institutions such as NATO and the Organization for Security and Cooperation in Europe (OSCE) to guarantee stability in the Balkans and the Transcaucasus, and continued exclusion from the EU, could also encourage Turkey's partial withdrawal. On the other hand, nationalism may also embrace the feeling of common belonging with peoples perceived to be from a similar cultural, historic and ethnic background. This shared sentiment could lead to a more activist policy towards such peoples. Turkey's relations with the newly independent Turkic states of the former Soviet Union must be considered in this context given the backdrop of recent developments in and around Turkey. Any shift in official circles towards ethnic nationalism could have serious repercussions in Turkey for the future of civic nationalism, which has been traditionally espoused by Turkish governments.[2]

2. For the use of the terms 'ethnic' and 'civic' nationalism see Anthony D. Smith, *National Identity* (Harmondsworth, Middlesex: Penguin, 1991).

The rapid unravelling of the Soviet Union was not expected by the leaderships in Ankara and Soviet Central Asia. With a few notable exceptions – Cyprus, Western Thrace, and the position of the Turkish minority in Bulgaria since the mid-1980s – Turkish officials had generally followed the policy established by Ataturk and had given little attention to the fate of the 'Turks' and Turkic peoples outside the Republic of Turkey. But with the independence of the Soviet republics, the sudden rediscovery of almost forgotten peoples of Turkic origin led to inflated hopes and unrealistic expectations on the part of some Turkish officials. Ankara's enthusiasm to develop and expand ties with the Transcaucasus and post-Soviet Central Asia was spurred on in part by Western governments, which feared the possible spread of Iranian influence in the region. Although the current Çiller government has adopted a more cautious and pragmatic approach towards post-Soviet Central Asia, the importance of Turkic solidarity is still emphasized, given the background of the upsurge of nationalist feeling in Turkey.

This study aims to examine the achievements and shortcomings of recent Turkish policy towards Uzbekistan, Kazakhstan, Turkmenistan and Kyrgyzstan, the newly independent Turkic states in Central Asia. Less attention is given to the more Iranian-oriented and largely Farsi-speaking Tajikistan, which has been torn by civil strife since 1992. This study will not focus on Turkey's very important political and strategic interests in the Transcaucasus *per se*, although relations between Turkey and Azerbaijan must be taken into account as they have had a bearing on Turkish policy towards post-Soviet Central Asia. The study asks how important Central Asia is for Turkey and Turkey for Central Asia and explores the impact of these ties on other interested regional actors.

After a short historical background the study focuses on the nature of Turkish involvement in the region in recent years. One chapter is devoted to Turkish economic interests. Another examines the extent of competition and cooperation between Turkey, Iran and Russia in post-Soviet Central Asia. In the conclusion, future possible courses of action for Turkey in the region are assessed, against the background of recent domestic developments in Turkey.

Terminology: 'Turkic' vs 'Turkish'

In Turkey politicians and commentators speak of the Turkish republics or Turkish-speaking republics when referring to former Soviet Central Asia. They regard many of the peoples of Central Asia as 'Turks' rather than peoples of ethnic Turkic origin. The intermingling between peoples of Turkic, Mongol and Persian ethnic stock in Central Asia is outlined in Chapter 2. The notion of a pure 'Turk' is thus a problematic one. Similarly, the Ottoman Turks intermixed with other peoples of the Balkans and the Middle East. The distinction between the terms 'Turkish' and 'Turkic' is not apparent in the Turkish language. In Turkey it is argued that the distinction is actually an artificial

3

one imposed by Western scholars to separate what is in fact a common people of Turkish origin.[3] In this study the term 'Turkish' is used with regard to the Turkish republic and nation. There are separate Turkish and Kazakh nations, for example, but both are ethnically Turkic. The term 'Turkic' is used here to refer to peoples who, in spite of intermarriage with other ethnic groups, believe that they are still able to trace a common ethnic origin. Initially, after the disintegration of the Soviet Union commentators in Turkey employed the terms 'Türki' and 'Türkik' rather than 'Türk' when speaking of the newly independent Central Asian states, thereby mirroring the Turkish–Turkic distinction in English. However, the term 'Turk' was soon universally adopted for the Central Asian states to emphasize the close relationship between them and Turkey.[4] Hence, in practice, in the Turkish language no distinction is made between the 'Outside Turks' of Central Asia (see pp. 7–8) and those of the Balkans, even though the latter still regard themselves as being part of a Turkish nation rather than constituting a separate nation of, say, Western Thrace Turks.

Difficulties in direct translation from Turkish to English mean that in this study the distinction between the terms 'Turkic' and 'Turkish' cannot always be rigidly applied. Hence, reference is made to the first and second Turkic rather than Turkish summits. To many Turks the designation 'Turkish' would sound more appropriate in these particular instances. The reader should remain mindful of the distinctions outlined above.

3. Interview with Seyfi Taşhan, Head of the Foreign Policy Research Institute of Turkey, Ankara, 6 December 1994.
4. Erol Mütercimler, *21 Yüzyılın Eşiğinde Uluslararası Sistem ve Türkiye-Türk Cumhuriyetleri İliskiler Modeli (The International System and the Model of Relations between Turkey and the Turkic Republics at the Threshold of the Twenty-First Century)* (Istanbul: Anahtar Kitaplar Yayınevi, 1993), pp. 19–21. One problem with the use of the term 'Türki' was that an Arabic suffix was added to a Turkish word. This was evidently not well received by many in Turkey.

2 HISTORICAL BACKGROUND

In the absence of accurate census figures, one can only estimate the total number of peoples of Turkic origin who currently live in the CIS. According to the Turkish Ministry of Culture, relying on 1989 Soviet census statistics, this total was over 49.5 million:[5] over 30 million concentrated in Central Asia, over 10 million in today's Russian Federation (around half of whom were Tatars) and almost 6 million Azerbaijanis in Azerbaijan. According to the same census the largest nations of ethnic Turkic origin in today's CIS (i.e. those with a population of over 5 million) were the Uzbeks (16,686,240), Kazakhs (8,137,878), Azerbaijanis (6,791,106) and Tatars (6,645,588). The smallest Turkic groups, according to the previous census, in 1979, were the Karaim of the Crimea and the Tofas of Siberia, who numbered approximately 3,000 and 800 respectively. Widely scattered across Central Asia, the Transcaucasus, Siberia and Moldova are Turkic peoples who are largely Sunni or (in the case of Azerbaijanis) Shiite Muslims, but there are, among others, also Orthodox Christian Chuvash, Orthodox Christian and Animist Yakuts, Jewish Heterodox Karaim and Buddhist and Animist Altayans.

Recent Turkish governments have focused on developing relations with the titular nations of the new independent states in the former Soviet Union. It is more problematic to foster ties with Turkic peoples who are minorities in other states, especially in the Russian Federation. In some cases not only are these Turkic peoples non-Muslim, but also their feeling of identity with Turkey may be much more tenuous, being based only on an obscure and distant past.

From an early age almost every Turkish schoolchild learns how, many centuries ago, Turks migrated in waves from the depths of eastern Asia to spread civilization across Central Asia, the Middle East and the Indian subcontinent. It seems that the first identifiable Turkic people can be traced back to the second millennium BC in territory around present-day Mongolia.[6] The Great Wall of China was built in the third century

---

5. *TDN*, 10 February 1992.

6. For good general works on the early history of the Turks in Central Asia, see Gavin Hambly (ed.), *Central Asia* (New York: Delacorte Press, 1969); and Jean-Paul Roux, 'Historical introduction', in Margaret Bainbridge (ed.), *The Turkic Peoples of the World* (London and New York: Kegan Paul International, 1993), pp. 1–30. See also Shirin Akiner, 'Post-Soviet Central Asia: past is prologue', in Peter Ferdinand (ed.), *The New Central Asia and its Neighbours* (London: RIIA/Pinter, 1994).

BC to keep at bay the fierce warriors of the Hsiung-nu, a Turkic people from which the later Huns were descended. Movements of other Turkic peoples followed the Huns and swept across the steppes and deserts of Central Asia in the period of Europe's Dark Ages. Some finally settled and carved out empires like that of the Uighurs in the eighth century. However, Iranian settlements across Central Asia predated by several centuries the original descent of the Huns in the region. In the eighth and ninth centuries the Arab conquest left the imprint of Islam on this territory. The Mongol hordes of Genghiz Khan subjugated the region in the early thirteenth century before intermingling with the Iranian and by now largely sedentarized Turkic peoples. In the late fourteenth century Timur (Tamerlane) briefly controlled Central Asia, Iran, Anatolia and parts of the Indian subcontinent, but his empire soon broke up, as did that of the so-called 'Golden Horde' (descendants of the earlier Mongol hordes of Genghiz Khan). By the mid-sixteenth century Muscovy had established a firm foothold in the region.

Central Asia had been a centre of prosperity until the decline of the Silk Route in the sixteenth century. Even under the Mongol warriors, culture, the arts and science flourished. It has been argued that the fruits of civilization were originally brought to Central Asia not by the Turks but by the Persians in the ninth and tenth centuries, and that the area remained under Persian cultural influence up to the nineteenth century.[7] Today, both Turks and Iranians base their interests in the territories of former Soviet Central Asia partly on historical and cultural grounds. In reality, however, through intermarriage between the various peoples of different ethnic stock, it became impossible to talk of pure Turks or Persians. According to another argument, ethnic groups in Central Asia were neither historically nor territorially based. In the absence of so-called 'spatial segregation', kings and sultans did not rule over territory as such but over people, and it was of little concern what language these people spoke as long as they demonstrated allegiance.[8]

The Muscovite Ivan the Terrible defeated the Tatar remnants of the Golden Horde at Kazan and Astrakhan in 1552 and 1556. This prompted the Ottoman Turks, who had come to power in Anatolia and seized Constantinople in 1453, to attempt to wrest from Muscovy control of these strategically important territories near the Don and Volga rivers. Hoping to open a channel between the Black Sea and Caspian Sea and maintain contacts with the Uzbeks beyond the Caspian, the Ottomans and their Tatar allies failed in their attempt to retake Astrakhan in 1569.[9] Thereafter, the Ottomans diverted their

7. See Shireen Hunter, 'Central Asia and the Middle East: patterns of interaction and influence', *Central Asia Monitor*, no. 6, 1992, p. 11.
8. Nazif Shahrani, 'The lessons and uses of history', *Central Asia Monitor*, no. 1, 1993, p. 25.
9. Carl Max Kortepeter, *Ottoman Imperialism During the Reformation: Europe and the Caucasus* (London and New York: University of London Press and New York University Press, 1972), pp. 28–30 and 90–91.

attention more towards the Balkans and the Middle East and had only minimal interaction with the Turkic peoples of Central Asia. The latter became divided under the Khanates of Khiva and Kokand and the Emirate of Bukhara until these in turn came into Russia's orbit by the late nineteenth century.

The Turks in the modern period

Renewed interest in the Turkic peoples of Central Asia only took hold in the Ottoman empire in the late nineteenth century with the emergence of Pan-Turkic thinking. Pan-Turkism was concerned with the establishment of some form of union of Turkic peoples. These ideas were introduced by Crimean Turks who had fled from Russia to the Ottoman empire to escape repression embodied in the policy of forced Russification and Christianization. After 1908 the Young Turks became increasingly attracted to Pan-Turkism. One of their early leaders, Enver Pasha, died in Central Asia in 1922, fighting to realize the Pan-Turkic dream at the side of the Basmachi rebels against communist rule imposed by Moscow. Although the Turkic peoples in what became the Soviet Union were unable to organize a concerted opposition to the communists, Stalin was anxious enough to introduce a deliberate policy of 'divide and rule' in 1924. New territorial administrative units were artificially created in Soviet Central Asia and national identities were manufactured for peoples such as the Kazakhs, Kyrgyz, Turkmen and Uzbeks, who until then had been barely aware of their collective and separate identities, being traditionally divided into hordes, clans and tribes.

In the interwar period, the original rapprochement between Ataturk and Lenin, Ataturk's distaste for Pan-Turkism, and his desire to consolidate the newly founded Republic of Turkey, led to Turkish officials largely ignoring the fate of the so-called Outside Turks (*'Dis Turkler'*), so long as there was no open discrimination against them. Before the foundation of the Turkish Republic, by Article 8 of the Treaty concluded between Soviet Russia and Ataturk and his supporters in March 1921, both sides agreed to 'forbid the formation or presence on their territory of organisations or groups claiming to be the government of the other country or part of the territory and also the presence of groups that have hostile intentions with regard to the other country'.[10] Ataturk thereby pledged not to support Pan-Turkic elements in Soviet Russia in return for Moscow's promise not to promote communism in the territory he controlled.

While promoting the concept of Anatolianism – the idea that the traditional homeland of the Turks was the territory known as Anatolia within the boundaries of the new

---

10. For the text of the treaty see Basil Dmytryshyn and Frederick Cox, *The Soviet Union and the Middle East – A Documentary Record of Afghanistan, Iran and Turkey 1917–1985* (Princeton, NJ: The Kingston Press, 1987), pp. 473–80.

Turkish Republic of 1923 – Ataturk and his historians also explained that many Turks had been forced to abandon their original, historic homeland in Central Asia because of the increasing desiccation of the area. There was an element of truth in this, but history was turned into myth when, seeking to consolidate a Turkish in place of an Ottoman identity, the historians referred to Central Asia as the cradle of Turkish – and, indeed, of every – civilization. The Balkans could not be used as a reference point after the failures of the Ottoman empire there. Stressing Central Asian roots could be regarded as a denial of the Ottoman heritage. Bearing in mind this interpretation of history, it was perhaps surprising that Ataturk and his successors displayed so little concern for their original homeland until the break-up of the Soviet Union.

Only fringe Pan-Turkic groups within the new Republic of Turkey were eager to cultivate close ties with the Outside Turks. At the time of the Second World War some Turkish officials may have been tempted by German promises to support the formation of a Turkic state around the Crimea and the Caspian Sea, if Ankara were to enter the war on the side of the Axis powers. The National Action Party of Alpaslan Türkeş continued to espouse Pan-Turkic goals after the war – for example, proposing at one time the waging of a Holy War against the Soviet Union to create an 'all-Turkish Union' – but it did not become a major force in Turkish politics. The pinnacle of this party's success was in elections in 1977 when it secured almost one million votes and won 16 seats in the legislature. Türkeş was able to tap into rising nationalist feeling at that time after the crisis in Cyprus and the imposition of the US arms embargo.[11]

Following on from the original Treaty of March 1921, the official Turkish line, which continued even throughout the Cold War period, sought to avoid antagonizing the Soviet Union. Hostility towards communism as an ideology discouraged serious study in Turkey of recent political and social developments in what had become communist Soviet Central Asia. However, Moscow still suspected that Turkish governments might try to rekindle Pan-Turkic thought in the Soviet Union and thus never allowed even the Turkish Communist Party to develop ties with Turkic Muslim communists. It was all the more surprising, then, that Moscow should allow Demirel, when Prime Minister, to visit Baku and Tashkent in September 1967, where he was received by large and enthusiastic crowds calling him *kardeş* (brother).[12] This visit received little attention in the Turkish press at the time and was not effectively followed up.

11. The most comprehensive treatment of the origins and development of Pan-Turkism in English is to be found in Jacob M. Landau, *Pan-Turkism in Turkey: A Study in Irredentism* (Hamden, CT: Archon Books, 1981).
12. Kemal H. Karpat, 'Turkish–Soviet relations', in Kemal H. Karpat (ed.), *Turkey's Foreign Policy in Transition, 1950–1974* (London: E.J. Brill, 1975), p. 103.

The Soviet Central Asians themselves, under the watchful eye of Moscow, had little opportunity to develop independent relations with the outside world in general and with Turkey in particular. Many Russian immigrants were encouraged to settle in Soviet Central Asia and the region became a major supplier of raw materials, especially cotton, for the rest of the Soviet Union. In return, Soviet Central Asia became dependent on manufactured goods from the more industrially advanced Soviet republics. Not until Moscow relaxed its control in the final months of Mikhail Gorbachev's presidency were the Central Asians able to establish their own contacts with other states and take the first tentative steps towards independence.

3 TURKEY AND THE BREAK-UP OF THE SOVIET UNION

The Gorbachev period

Even before Gorbachev assumed power, relations between Turkey and the Soviet Union were improving, as was demonstrated by the conclusion of the landmark Natural Gas Agreement of September 1984. From 1987 onwards the Soviet Union agreed to deliver natural gas to meet Turkey's energy needs for the next 25 years through a pipeline across Romania and Bulgaria. In part-payment Moscow agreed to import Turkish goods and cover the cost of Turkish construction workers in the Soviet Union. As a result bilateral trade turnover almost quadrupled from $476 million in 1987 to $1.8 billion in 1990. This trade was of a complementary nature, with Turkey importing primarily gas and oil and exporting pharmaceuticals, plastics, leather goods, iron and steel products and agricultural goods. The Turkish Eximbank extended credits worth over $1 billion to boost trade with the Soviet Union and cover the extra costs of Turkish construction workers. Presidents Turgut Özal and Gorbachev signed a Treaty of Friendship and Good Neighbourliness in Moscow in March 1991. On that occasion both sides pledged to increase their trade turnover to $10 billion by the end of the decade. With the end of the Soviet Union, Turkey and Russia made a similar pledge after Russia agreed to continue the operation of the Natural Gas Agreement.

The increasing importance of economic ties with Moscow, support for Gorbachev's domestic reforms, and traditional Turkish concern not to be seen to be interfering in the internal affairs of the Soviet Union accounted for the restraint of the Turkish government in January 1990 when Soviet troops entered Baku. Withstanding pressure from its own population to give some form of active support to their co-ethnics, Ankara remained quiet as Soviet armed forces brutally repressed the activities of the Azerbaijani Popular Front after extensive mob violence against the Armenian minority in Baku.

As part of Gorbachev's reforms, individual Soviet republics were given limited freedom to conduct a foreign policy of sorts. In the second half of 1990 the Central Asian republics, in line with other republics, issued declarations of sovereignty. In practice this did not challenge the right of Moscow to make important decisions on their behalf, but a number of relatively low-level delegations from Soviet Central Asia were now free to tour Turkey and *vice versa* to discuss matters related to such issues as culture, science, telecommunications, health and the economy.

Higher-level diplomatic exchanges commenced with the visit of President Özal to the Soviet Union in March 1991. Özal and his large, mainly commercial, entourage were not only received in Moscow, but also travelled to Azerbaijan, Kazakhstan and Ukraine. Ties with Ukraine were being cultivated in order to realize a separate Turkish project – the Black Sea Economic Cooperation organization, which was formally inaugurated in 1992. In Kazakhstan, Özal concluded agreements on scientific-technical cooperation and cultural exchange, discussed the possibility of Turkish assistance to restructure the Kazakh economy, and talked of opening direct flights between Almaty and Istanbul. None of these issues was of a sensitive nature to Moscow. Özal's visit led in turn to the arrival of higher-ranking Soviet Central Asian delegations in Turkey. In May 1991 the Prime Minister of Kyrgyzstan was welcomed; he was followed the next month by the Tajik President, who attended the meeting of the World Economic Forum in Istanbul.

A decisive turning-point was the failure of the coup attempt by hardliners against Gorbachev in August 1991, which accelerated the break-up of the Soviet Union. Even the Soviet Central Asian leaderships came to realize that the days of the Soviet Union were numbered. They followed the example of other republics and declared their independence. The Kazakh authorities, however, refused to take this step, not wishing to alarm the republic's very large Russian minority. Nevertheless, the failure of the coup gave heightened significance to the visit of the Kazakh leader Nursultan Nazarbaev to Turkey at the end of September 1991. This was originally intended to be a mere courtesy visit, but Nazarbaev's agreement with his hosts to sign a Joint Declaration of Principles and Aims now assumed new significance. Agreement was also made to set up a joint consultative mechanism and the establishment of interparliamentary ties was to be given serious consideration. Turkey promised to extend a Turkish Eximbank credit of $10 million. Now able to negotiate on more points of detail, the two sides discussed the possibility of Turkey importing coal from Kazakhstan in return for the sale of consumer and electrical goods.[13] At around the same time two official Turkish fact-finding missions were despatched to the Transcaucasus and Central Asia to assess the conditions there. They reported that the republics were eager to expand trade, set up joint ventures and send students and personnel to Turkey for training.[14] These missions did not, however, recommend that Turkey should recognize the declarations of independence of the republics.

13. *TDN*, 27 and 30 September 1991.
14. *Ibid.*, 3 October 1991.

Finally, Ankara and Baku agreed to establish formal diplomatic ties. Under pressure from public opinion in Turkey and Azerbaijan, eager to pre-empt possible Iranian diplomatic recognition of Azerbaijan, and aware perhaps that they had acted too cautiously in January 1990, the Turkish authorities decided to recognize Azerbaijani independence on 9 November 1991. The Central Asians still had to wait. At the beginning of December, Ankara politely turned down the request of visiting President Saparmurad Niyazov to recognize the independence of Turkmenistan. Instead, it was agreed to establish consulates-general; a Friendship and Cooperation Treaty and several economic agreements were also signed.

The formation of the CIS

The formation of the CIS on 8 December 1991, and the decision of the Soviet Central Asian republics to join it after a summit meeting in Ashgabat three days later, to all intents and purposes marked the dissolution of the Soviet Union, although this was not officially acknowledged for several more days. Before this acknowledgment, on 16 December, the Turkish government announced that in principle it was ready to establish diplomatic relations with all the independent republics; Ankara was eager not to convey the impression that it was only interested in developing ties with the Turkic republics. The same day Uzbek President Islam Karimov was in Turkey on an official visit to sign various agreements, including one outlining the Principles and Aims of Relations between the two states and another which referred to the opening of consulates in both countries' capitals. In spite of the sudden decision to conclude full diplomatic relations with Uzbekistan, it was some time before Turkey could open embassies in Tashkent and other Central Asian capitals; instead the Turkish embassy in Moscow coordinated Turkey's relations with the former Soviet republics.

Presidents Askar Akayev of Kyrgyzstan and Ayaz Mutalibov of Azerbaijan also visited Ankara, in December 1991 and January 1992 respectively, to conclude Treaties of Friendship and Cooperation. In what was becoming a whirlwind of diplomatic activity, Turkish Foreign Minister Hikmet Çetin toured all the newly independent Central Asian states and Ukraine in February–March 1992. Less than two months later Prime Minister Demirel was welcomed in former Soviet Central Asia.

These dramatic developments led to what seems to have been a feeling of euphoria shared by the Turkish public and officialdom alike. The Turks suddenly believed that they were not alone in the world but that there were after all other 'Turks' living in the former Soviet Union. It was imagined and hoped that in embracing these other Turks, Turkey's stature in the world order would be elevated accordingly. This feeling of exhilaration came hard on the heels of the realization that Turkey would not join the EC in the foreseeable future, after the negative Brussels response to Turkey's application in December 1989. The worsening Kurdish problem had also been lowering morale.[15] Commentaries in the local media at the time further stirred up Turkish pride and nationalist fervour.

Excitement was clearly apparent in the two parliamentary debates convened on 12 and 17 December 1991 to discuss how Turkey should proceed in its relations with the Turkic republics. Not surprisingly, the debates in both cases were introduced by a mellowed Alpaslan Türkeş. On each occasion Türkeş warned that Ankara should act quickly before other interested states such as Iran, Saudi Arabia, Germany and the United States could steal an advantage over the Turks. Somewhat inflating his figures, Türkeş declared that there were now 200 million Turks in the world who spoke Turkish (the number of people who speak one of the Turkic languages is probably around 150 million). Another deputy from the governing True Path Party took the opportunity to press enthusiastically for the formation of a new ministry responsible for the Outside Turks (such a ministry has still not been created).[16]

This initial feeling of euphoria was also encouraged by officials both in the West and in former Soviet Central Asia itself. Western political leaders were clearly anxious to prevent the possible expansion of Iranian influence in the region and were thus eager to urge Ankara to play a leading role there. For example, in Moscow in February 1992 NATO Secretary-General Manfred Wörner declared that NATO looked to Turkey to support the Western alliance's interests in Central Asia and to counter the danger of Islamic fundamentalism spreading there.[17] When visiting Ankara in December 1991 both Karimov and Akayev were full of praise for their hosts and made impassioned pleas for their support. Karimov declared that he looked up to Turkey as an elder brother (*ağabey*) and noted that Uzbekistan and the other newly independent Central Asian states had a lot to learn from Ankara. He stressed that Uzbekistan urgently needed economic, political and cultural assistance from Turkey.[18] Days later Akayev likened Turkey to the morning star which was guiding the paths of the Turkic republics.[19]

---

15. These feelings were depicted by the Turkish journalist Cengiz Çandar in his '*Değişmekte olan Dünyada Türkiye'nin Bağımsızlığını Kazanan Yeni Türk Cumhuriyetlerle İlişkileri*' ('Turkey's relations with the newly independent Turkic states in a changing world'), in Sabahattin Şen (ed.), *Yeni Dünya Düzeni ve Türkiye (The New World Order and Turkey)* (Istanbul: Baglam Yayıncılık, 1992), pp. 133–42.

16. For full details of the two parliamentary debates see *Türkiye Büyük Millet Meclisi Tutanak Dergısı, Donem 19, Yasama Yili 1: Cilt 1 1991, 1–16 (Official Records of the Turkish Grand National Assembly, Period 19, Legislative Year 1, Vol. 1 1991, 1–16)*, pp. 559–87 and 609–40.

17. Ahmed Rashid, *The Resurgence of Central Asia: Islam or Nationalism* (Karachi: Oxford University Press, and London and New Jersey: Zed Books, 1994), p. 210. Just before the visit of Secretary of State James Baker to Central Asia in February 1992, a senior US administration official declared that the United States hoped that the Central Asians would look to Europe and secular Turkey for guidance and 'strategic orientation' rather than to other neighbours like Iran. See *Los Angeles Times*, 10 February 1992.

18. *Cumhuriyet* (in Turkish), 20 December 1991.

19. *TDN*, 24 December 1991.

These were illustrative of other similar statements made by key Central Asian statesmen at that time.

With the benefit of hindsight, Western analysts have tended to argue that these statements were calculated to placate Ankara, and that a new *ağabey* was actually what the Central Asians least desired after their experiences with Moscow. However, one should not forget that in December 1991 the Central Asians were almost desperate for Turkish support for the recognition of their independence and for assistance in publicizing this to the world at large. Indeed, there is hardly any doubt that the Central Asian leaders themselves were at least in part stirred by feelings of what was an admittedly long-forgotten sense of Turkic solidarity.

In the initial flush of excitement produced by the unravelling of the Soviet Union, and actually having little knowledge or experience of dealing with the Soviet Central Asians, officials in Ankara seem at first to have overestimated their capability to affect political, social and economic developments in the newly independent Turkic states. The so-called 'Turkish model' of a secular state and liberal democracy with a free market economy was not easy to adopt. The Central Asian economies had become heavily dependent on Moscow and the close infrastructural links that this entailed could not be readily disentangled. There was no tradition of democracy in former Soviet Central Asia. Even in the communist era, authority was based on a complex network of hordes, clans and tribes and regional power centres. Local communist leaders found it relatively easy to don a new nationalist mantle, although there was a danger that heightened nationalist feeling would aggravate more deep-rooted tribal and regional rivalries. In contrast to the Baltic states, Soviet Central Asian leaderships and publics had had independence thrust upon them. Eager to continue to enjoy the benefits of subsidies from Moscow, over 90% of the Central Asian population voted in favour of Gorbachev's Draft Union Treaty in the referendum of March 1991. Even after the failed coup attempt, the Central Asian leaderships still held out hope for the maintenance of a form of economic union.

Before the demise of the Soviet Union friction between the peoples of Central Asia had become more clearly apparent. Superimposed on traditional divisions in Central Asian society, the gradual emergence of new nationalist feeling encouraged by the official policy of glasnost, at a time of serious unemployment and a severe shortage of housing and land, became an explosive combination. There was violence against immigrants from the Caucasus in Kazakhstan, Tajikistan and Uzbekistan in 1989 and 1990, as well as waves of intra-Turkic strife. One of the worst incidents took place in June 1989, when large numbers of Meskhetian Turks had to be airlifted from the Ferghana Valley, after over a hundred were slaughtered by local Uzbek bands. A year later in the Osh region of Kyrgyzstan Soviet troops again had to intervene, this time to separate Krygyz and Uzbeks after more than 800 fatalities were reported; Turkic solidarity was obviously not necessarily an instinctive feeling. Alarmed by this escalating violence, the Central Asian leaderships addressed the problem in summit meetings in Almaty and Tashkent in June 1990 and August 1991.

Officials in Ankara may be hoping that an appeal to common 'primordial' ethnic ties could help to smooth the process of national formation in Central Asia, but according to the Kyrgyz Foreign Minister, for example, the conflicts in the Osh region subsided not because of any shared Turkic sentiment but rather because of common religious bonds and the good sense of the Uzbek and Kyrgyz leaderships.[20]

The original high hopes and expectations in Turkey for a close development of relations with the newly independent Turkic states eventually had to be revised after the disappointment of the first Turkic Summit convened in Ankara at the end of October 1992 (described in greater detail in Chapter 4). Turkish officials realized that in spite of an initial genuine enthusiasm to build up ties with Turkey, the Central Asian leaders were anxious not to antagonize Russia and were also interested in expanding contacts with states other than Turkey that were prepared to offer them support.

20. Interview with Dr Rosa Otunbayeva, the Foreign Minister of Kyrgyzstan, Istanbul, 22 September 1994. In another demonstration of a lack of Turkic solidarity, permission for a group of persecuted Meskhetian Turks to settle in Turkey was not granted until July 1992. The Turkish government had been encountering serious difficulties in accommodating large numbers of refugees from Bulgaria and northern Iraq.

4 THE EMERGENCE OF A 'GIGANTIC "TURKISH" WORLD'? THE ROAD TO THE FIRST TURKIC SUMMIT

The term 'Pan-Turkism' should be employed with great caution. As noted above, in essence it refers to any form of union of peoples of Turkic origin. In practice, the term is commonly understood to entail the ultimate goal of the political unity of Turkic peoples – a Turkic Empire. It is thus associated in the eyes of many with aggressive expansionism. Recent Turkish governments have been particularly mindful of the pejorative nature of the term and have been eager to emphasize that their policies are in no way connected with so-called Pan-Turkic goals. There are still extremist groups in Turkey and, indeed, in Central Asia who advocate what is in effect this extreme, political form of Pan-Turkism. However, could the term not also be employed to depict a form of cultural union of Turkic peoples? This more moderate form of Pan-Turkism could have as an ultimate objective the establishment of a Turkic Commonwealth. Türkeş and his followers appear to have opted now to pursue this goal of cultural Pan-Turkism, and other agencies and individuals in Turkey seem to be attracted towards this objective.

According to officials at the Turkish Ministry of Foreign Affairs, Turkey has never sought to shape some form of commonwealth or union with the newly independent Turkic states of the former Soviet Union. Turkey's intention was rather only to deepen cooperation by establishing various fora in which issues of common concern could be freely discussed.[21] However, the record indicates that key Turkish politicians may have hoped – and indeed may still be hoping – to establish a much more institutionalized form of cooperation, perhaps along the lines of the kind of Turkic Commonwealth or cultural union now advocated by Türkeş.

In this context it is interesting to note the differing views of scholars from Turkey, the then Soviet Union and Western Europe who attended a major symposium held in Bodrum, Turkey in September 1991. One panelist advocated the creation of a Turkestan Federation of the Turkic Republics of the Soviet Union. Another contended that a Union of Turkic States should be established between the republics based on the model of

---

21. Interview with an official in the Turkish Ministry of Foreign Affairs responsible for former Soviet Central Asia, Ankara, 6 December 1994.

European integration. One commentator was prepared to include Turkey and Tajikistan within a future cultural and economic entity called a Turkestan Confederation.[22] No one was prepared to press for a Turkic Empire. In each of these scenarios Turkey would either be excluded or would only play a supporting role. The panelists were not able to envisage that only three months later politicians from Turkey and Central Asia alike would be urging Turkey to be at the forefront of a 'Turkish/Turkic' world.

Several Pan-Turkic conferences were assembled outside Turkey. In April 1991 a 'Turkic Peoples' Convention', convened in Kazan in Tatarstan, declared its aim to be the revision of the 'ideology of Turkism' among 'Turkic' peoples. A 'Turkish' Fund was created to support the development of 'Turkic peoples' in the Soviet Union.[23] In January 1992 the Kazakhstan Democratic Party organized a Pan-Turkic conference in Almaty. The participants appealed for the establishment of a 'Turkic state' stretching from Kazan to Almaty (obviously excluding Turkey). As a first step a Coordination Council was formed.[24] These initiatives appear to have been still-born and did not receive official Turkish support. It would seem that Ankara was determined to steer clear from such movements over which it could have little control. Moreover, open support for these groups would only aggravate Moscow. Turkish officials must also be aware that extremist Pan-Turkic groups are not popular in Central Asia and that their activities are closely monitored and sometimes repressed by governments. Some of these groups are also closely connected with radical Islamic factions. In Uzbekistan, for instance, the small 'Turkestan' group has been driven underground. The much larger but also persecuted Birlik movement has within its ranks those who are attracted to Pan-Turkism in its various guises.

In what has become a notorious speech, the usually cautious Demirel, when Prime Minister, declared in February 1992 that with the disintegration of the Soviet Union a 'gigantic "Turkish" world' was currently being formed, stretching from the Adriatic Sea to the Great Wall of China.[25] This speech was seized upon by those critical of Turkey – for instance, the Bosnian Serb leader Radovan Karadzic – as supposed evidence of the Turkish government's Pan-Turkic policy. In another surprise, Demirel included Türkeş within his large delegation which toured Central Asia at the end of April 1992. On this trip Demirel was compelled to counter charges that he was pursuing a Pan-Turkic policy. In Kyrgyzstan he stressed that 'We consider Turks as a great big family,

22. See the presentations by Ahmet Nahmedov, Baymirza Hayıt and Timur Kocaoğlu in *Yeni Forum– Türkiye Modeli ve Türk Kökenli Cumhuriyetlerle eski Sovyet Halkları (Yeni Forum – The Turkish Model, the Turkic Republics and the Former Soviet Peoples)* (Ankara: Yeni Forum, 1992).
23. *TDN*, 26 April 1991, and *Cumhuriyet*, 13 June 1991.
24. *Cumhuriyet*, 23 January 1992.
25. *Ibid.*, 24 February 1992.

but we are not Pan-Turkic'.[26] In Kazakhstan Demirel gave assurances that Turkey had no Pan-Turkic aspirations, but noted that there was nothing wrong in Turks in Turkey declaring that Central Asia was the land of their forefathers and that their culture and history originated there.[27] Even after the disappointment of the first Turkic Summit, in February 1993 – admittedly addressing the ultra-nationalist 'Turkish Clubs' Association (*Turk Ocaklari*) in Ankara – Demirel referred to Central Asia and Azerbaijan as a new Eurasian Community populated by Turks. He added that Turkey would not administer these Turks but would 'lead them to the world'.[28]

Did Demirel have in mind here the creation of some form of Turkic Commonwealth? Certainly, again on his Central Asian tour in the spring of 1992, the Turkish Prime Minister referred to the prospects of forming an 'association of independent Turkic states' which would not be 'dominated' by Turkey. On this occasion Demirel also noted that 'after their experience with the Soviet Union they [the Central Asians] would not accept the domination of another big brother'.[29] Türkeş was more specific concerning how this association should be structured. He proposed that a High Council of Turkic Republics composed of presidents, prime ministers and foreign ministers could meet several times a year under a rotating presidency.[30] In the aftermath of the first Turkic Summit, leading Turkish academics still felt able to advocate the formation of a Community of 'Turkish' Republics based on military, political, economic and cultural grounds.[31] Significantly, when visiting Moscow in September 1993, the new Turkish Prime Minister Tansu Çiller reportedly criticized Demirel's past use of slogans which referred to an enlarged Turkish world, noting that such pronunciations had undermined the trust between Turkey and Russia.[32]

Many Turkish officials must have realized that the formation of a Turkic Commonwealth was not possible in the foreseeable future after the disappointing results of the first Turkic Summit in Ankara in October 1992.[33] This meeting was attended by the heads

26. *TDN*, 30 April 1992.
27. *Ibid.*, 1 May 1992.
28. *Ibid.*, 24 February 1993.
29. *Ibid.*, 4 May 1992.
30. *Ibid.*, 11 June 1992.
31. See for example, Erol Manisalı, 'Uluslararası İlişkilerdeki Değişmeler "Türk Cumhuriyetleri Topluluğu'nu" Gerektırmektedir' ('Changes in international relations require a "Community of Turkic Republics" '), in Erol Manisalı (ed.), *Türk Cumhuriyetleri Arasında Politik ve Ekonomik İşbirliği, Uluslararası Girne Konferansları (Political and Economic Cooperation between the Turkic Republics, The International Girne Conference)* (Istanbul: Kıbrıs Araştırmaları Vakfı, 1993), pp. 5–6.
32. *Hürriyet* (in Turkish), 9 September 1993.
33. For full details of the first Turkic Summit, see the issues of *TDN*, *Cumhuriyet* and *Hürriyet* between 31 October and 4 November 1992; and also *Turkey Confidential*, no. 34, December 1992, p. 20. For the text of the Ankara Declaration (in Turkish) released at the end of the Summit, see *Cumhuriyet*, 1 November 1992.

of state from Turkey, Kyrgyzstan, Turkmenistan, Uzbekistan, Kazakhstan and Azerbaijan. Interestingly, Tajikistan was also originally invited to attend, but the civil war there led to the Tajik delegation failing to appear. It was perhaps not surprising that Tajik officials had been invited. Ambassador Bilal Şimşir, the Director-General of Relations with the CIS within the Turkish Ministry of Foreign Affairs, had grouped Tajikistan together with the Turkic states of the former Soviet Union in an article he had written earlier, on the grounds that over one-third of the Tajik population were 'Turkish' (i.e. the Uzbeks), and that because the Tajiks were predominantly Sunni and not Shiite Muslims they regarded themselves as being much closer to Turkey than to Iran.[34]

The authorities in Ankara, it seems, had not properly consulted with their Central Asian counterparts before the first Turkic Summit assembled. The intention was to conclude the Summit with the release of a Political Declaration, an Economic Declaration and a Press Communiqué. In his opening speech, President Özal, always the visionary, boldly announced that the twenty-first century would be the century of the Turks. Özal declared that a Turkic Common Market and a Turkic Development and Investment Bank should be established. He also pressed for firm commitments from Kazakhstan, Uzbekistan and Turkmenistan to agree to the construction of oil and gas pipelines from their territories to Europe via Turkey. This final point was bound to be opposed by Moscow. At that time Russian officials wanted to ensure that all pipelines would continue to cross Russian territory in order to maintain economic and political influence over the Central Asians.

Conclusions of the Summit

The first Turkic Summit eventually concluded with the publication of only one text, the Ankara Declaration. This spoke in vague and general terms of the need to develop cooperation in the fields of culture, education, language, security, the economy, and judicial and parliamentary affairs. A number of working groups were to be set up to study projects on economic and cultural development. It was decided to hold another Turkic Summit in Baku one year later, in line with an agreement to hold such meetings on a regular basis. A Protocol between Turkey and Turkmenistan was also concluded, envisaging the construction of a natural gas pipeline from Turkmenistan to Turkey (although the route such a pipeline would take was not specified). Turkish officials agreed, in addition, to construct a new terminal at Ashgabat airport.

34. Bilal N. Şimşir, 'Turkey's relations with the Central Asian Turkic republics (1989–1992)', *Turkish Review Quarterly Digest*, vol. 6, no. 28, summer 1992, p. 11. Note the surprising use of the term 'Turkic' and not 'Turkish' in this title.

The Ankara Declaration made no reference to the formation of a Turkic Common Market or Turkic Bank. The participants also made no firm pledges with regard to the construction of new oil pipelines. Karimov stated that he was opposed to the setting up of a supranational mechanism to coordinate the Turkic world. Nazarbaev, ever mindful of the substantial Russian population in Kazakhstan, was prepared to veto any declaration which referred to the formation of organizations based on purely religious or ethnic grounds. No press communiqué was issued because Nazarbaev also evidently refused to sign a statement implying the recognition of the Turkish Republic of Northern Cyprus as an independent state – this was apparently the only occasion on which Turkish officials have pressed the Central Asians for such recognition. It seems that the Kazakh President was concerned that parallels could be drawn between the position of the Russian minority in Kazakhstan and that of the Turks in Cyprus. In another demonstration of the lack of Turkic solidarity, the Ankara Declaration made no reference whatsoever to the Nagorno-Karabakh dispute, although Turkey and Azerbaijan must have been pressing for a statement critical of Armenia. It seems that the Central Asians were reluctant to antagonize Moscow. Russia and Armenia were in the process of developing closer links in the security sphere. Indeed, Russia, Armenia (but not Azerbaijan at that time) and the Central Asian states with the exception of Turkmenistan had signed the Tashkent Collective Security Treaty of May 1992. In practice, however, the Tashkent Treaty was interpreted to apply only in cases of aggression committed by states outside the former Soviet Union.

Quite clearly Turkish politicians had made a series of miscalculations. It seems they had failed to realize that much had changed since December 1991. For instance, by mid-1992 Russia had begun to focus its attention more on the problems of the 'near abroad' and was not prepared to abandon the approximately 10 million Russians living in former Soviet Central Asia. After the recent experience in Afghanistan, the leaderships in both Moscow and the Central Asian states were also fearful of the danger of radicalized Islam. Witnessing the deteriorating situation in Tajikistan, the Central Asians were willing to remain part of a Russian security umbrella. They also wished to remain part of the rouble zone in order to continue to benefit from at least an indirect Russian subsidization of their economy. It was thus in the interests of the Central Asians to remain sensitive to Russian fears of Pan-Turkism. These fears were in part irrational, based on deep-rooted historical animosities between the Russians and the Turks. In part, though, they were also manipulated by Russian policy-makers to keep in check the rising extremist nationalist forces in Russia. One should keep these distinctions in mind when, for instance, assessing statements such as that of Sergei Stankevich, Yeltsin's political adviser in mid-1992. Stankevich was on record as saying that Turkey could become the 'leader of a union stretching into Central Asia which could become a serious factor for the world'.[35]

35. *Guardian Weekly*, 5 July 1992.

20

It also seems that by October 1992 the newly independent Central Asian states had already become more confident of their position in the world. They no longer felt dependent on Turkey's support, although officials in Ankara had evidently earlier assisted the inexperienced Central Asians in the technicalities of applying for membership to major international organizations, and had helped expedite their entry into the Organization of Islamic Conference (OIC) and Economic Cooperation Organization (ECO). Becoming aware of the limited economic resources at Turkey's disposal, the Central Asians were more prepared to look elsewhere for additional economic and political backing. Thus, immediately after the first Turkic Summit, Nazarbaev was welcomed in Tehran to open up talks on commercial cooperation with his Iranian hosts.

However, although expectations in Ankara would need to be revised, it was also obvious that by October 1992 Turkey had already expended considerable resources and had an important stake in developments in Central Asia. Neither the Central Asians nor the Turks were prepared to abandon the close ties they had cultivated. Moreover, with the fires of Turkish nationalism being further fuelled by the crisis in the Balkans and difficulties in southeastern Turkey, Ankara was in no position suddenly to downplay the importance of common ethnic Turkic bonds.

5 BOTH SENTIMENT AND SELF-INTEREST: THE ROAD TO THE SECOND TURKIC SUMMIT

An important article on Turkey and its relations with the newly independent Turkic states, noting the shortcomings of the first Turkic Summit and referring to the initial ignorance of Turkey and the West concerning the problems of Central Asia, suggests that there has been a noticeable shift in Turkish policy towards the region from one based on sentiment – on 'fanciful notions of ethnic solidarity' – to one based more on self-interest.[36] It does seem that Turkish policy-makers were forced to make a sober reassessment of their policies towards the region, given the original exaggerated expectations and inflated hopes. But sentiment can prove to be durable. Sentiment and self-interest are not mutually exclusive, and a foreign policy can be based on both in varying proportions. The development of cultural and economic ties can strengthen links with the Turkic states, boost Turkey's international profile, and result in economic benefits for Turkey in the longer term.

The exacerbation of the Kurdish problem in Turkey in recent years is having an important impact on the Turkish domestic scene. In the face of increasing criticism from Western governments and human rights organizations, the Çiller government has almost made it a point of honour that outside elements should not interfere in the internal affairs of Turkey. The inability of these same governments and organizations to bring an end to the suffering in Bosnia has only hardened the resolve of the Turkish authorities. The Çiller government is also determined to halt the march to power of the more anti-Western, nationalist-Islamicist Welfare Party which triumphed in local elections in Istanbul, Ankara and many other municipalities in the spring of 1994. In these circumstances the Çiller government is adopting a course which appears increasingly close to that put forward by the advocates of ethnic nationalism.

In reality, Türkeş and his National Action Party have been providing the government with stauncher support than the Social Democrats (Çiller's official coalition partner), although at the time of writing the Social Democrats had agreed to merge with the

---

36. Philip Robins, 'Between sentiment and self-interest: Turkey's policy towards Azerbaijan and the Central Asian states', *Middle East Journal*, vol. 47, no. 4, autumn 1993, pp. 593–610.

opposition Republican People's Party, thus casting more doubt on the future of the Çiller coalition government. It is significant to note, though, that until his resignation in November 1994 after a personal clash with Çiller, the Social Democrat Mümtaz Soysal, foreign minister since the summer of 1994, had initiated an 'honourable' foreign policy which was more critical of the West than that of his predecessors. In the current domestic and international environment, nationalist sentiment is a potent motivating element in Turkish foreign policy. No Turkish government, therefore, is able to adopt a dismissive line towards the notions of Turkic brotherhood and solidarity.

Following the visits of the then Foreign Minister Çetin and Prime Minister Demirel to Central Asia in February and April 1992, there has been an interchange of diplomatic visits at various levels between Turkey and the newly independent Turkic states. In July 1992 Çetin toured Central Asia again together with Catherine Lalumière, the Secretary-General of the Council of Europe. Turkey at that time held the term presidency of the Council of Europe. Shortly before his death President Özal visited the region once more in April 1993, although this visit was overshadowed by the news of the intensification of hostilities around Nagorno-Karabakh and Özal's condemnation of the Armenians while on tour. In October 1994 President Demirel was received in Turkmenistan on the occasion of the third anniversary of Turkmenistan's independence. He also participated in an official ceremony to inaugurate – albeit only symbolically – the construction of a natural gas pipeline which was intended to connect Turkmenistan, Iran, Turkey and Central Europe. In view of the civil war in Tajikistan, Dushanbe was not included in any of the above travel itineraries after the first Çetin visit, although a Friendship and Cooperation Treaty between Turkey and Tajikistan was signed when the Tajik Vice-President was received in Ankara in July 1993. Perhaps surprisingly, even though she made an important trip to Moscow in September 1993, Çiller has yet to visit Central Asia since becoming Prime Minister. The diplomatic traffic from Central Asia to Turkey has been equally impressive, although the leaders of the Turkic states could not again assemble collectively in Turkey until October 1994, when the much-delayed second Turkic Summit was finally convened, not in Baku but in Istanbul.

In spite of this impressive consolidation of diplomatic contacts, Turkish policy towards post-Soviet Central Asia has not been an unmitigated success. In addition to the problems of the first Turkic Summit, Turkish officials have on other occasions made errors. For example, on his first tour of the region Çetin was briefed to inform his hosts that Turkey was prepared to represent the Central Asians in international fora and that Turkish embassies were willing to represent the interests of the Central Asian states. Only Uzbekistan accepted the Turkish offer. The other states, eager to project their independence and sovereignty, may have been offended by the Turkish offer. On this occasion the Central Asians also rejected Turkey's offer to provide them with books in the Latin alphabet on the grounds that they had not formally decided to replace the Cyrillic alphabet.[37]

One apparent trump card that officials in Ankara were eager to play was the ostensible relevance of the so-called Turkish model for the newly independent Turkic states. As has been noted, Western officials were particularly anxious that the Central Asians should take Turkey rather than Iran as their model. Demirel even submitted draft constitutions to the leaders of Uzbekistan, Kazakhstan and Kyrgyzstan for their consideration while he was in Central Asia in the spring of 1992. However, in practice, with the possible exception of Kyrgyzstan, the Central Asian leaderships seem to be more inclined to adopt a Chinese model of economic reform without real political democratization. With regard to Azerbaijan, the Turkish authorities were forced to perform a diplomatic *volte face* in the summer of 1993 and swiftly abandon the legitimately elected President Abulfaz Elchibey after he had been ousted from power by renegade military forces. Ankara's professed support for the value and relevance of a Turkish model of economic and political development for the newly independent Turkic states sounded increasingly hollow. In reality, no model may be imposed. Turkish officials were also sensitive, however, to the possible charges that Turkey was seeking to interfere in the internal affairs of other states.

In the case of Uzbekistan, for instance, Turkish officials apparently had to deal with official complaints concerning the granting of asylum to Muhammed Salih, the leader of the opposition Erk movement. This may have led to the recall of the Uzbek ambassador from Ankara in the summer of 1994: although the Turkish government declared that this action was due to drastic austerity measures in Uzbekistan, Salih alleged that the ambassador was withdrawn because he had become too sympathetic towards Turkey. The Uzbek opposition leader also stated that 1,780 of the 2,000 Uzbek students studying in Turkey might be withdrawn, as President Karimov was afraid of their prolonged exposure to a democratic regime! Certainly, Karimov's visit to Ankara in June 1994 was tension-ridden. The Uzbek President urged both Turkey and Uzbekistan to ensure that 'third parties' would not spoil their bilateral ties. Unlike on his previous visit in December 1991, Karimov made no reference to the 'Turkish model' and looked visibly uneasy when President Demirel gave a detailed account of the amount of credits, loans and humanitarian aid which Uzbekistan had received from Turkey since 1991.[38] A new Uzbek ambassador finally arrived in Ankara only one day before the second Turkic Summit.

37. *TDN*, 28 March 1992.
38. *Turkish Probe*, no. 84, 1 July 1994, p. 16.

Practical measures of support

Relative to the size of its economy, Turkey has offered considerable financial support, humanitarian assistance and technical aid to the newly independent Turkic states. Both sentiment and self-interest may account for the scale of these activities. Details of Turkey's economic involvement in the region will be discussed in the following chapter. This involvement is closely connected with Turkey's support for the development of infrastructure, telecommunications and transportation in the region. Turkey has also provided assistance, for example in the fields of education, the training of personnel in various occupations, military cooperation and religion. The Turkish Agency for Technical and Economic Cooperation (TIKA) has been responsible for helping to coordinate activities in the public and private sectors in the development field. Established in 1992, this agency has worked closely with international bodies such as the United Nations Development Programme (UNDP), the OECD and the World Health Organization (WHO). In an interview conducted in August 1994 the head of TIKA, Umut Arık, outlined the extensive activities of his agency in post-Soviet Central Asia. These included help in the improvement of banking systems, training personnel to operate in a market economy, establishing a computer network to link up research institutes with centres in Turkey, creating a Eurasian Union of Chambers of Commerces, and founding Turkic unions of news agencies, authors and university rectors. However, Arık did indicate that his agency required more financial support from the Turkish government. Revealing that TIKA was currently receiving only TL 300 billion, Arık noted that in the next few years his agency would need TL 4 trillion from the government.[39]

In order to facilitate business relations Turkish companies such as Netaş, Teletaş and the state-controlled PTT (General Directorate of Post, Telegraph and Telephones) have been active in installing and developing new telephone exchange systems in the Turkic states.[40] Through a link with the French-built satellite TÜRKSAT 2, the Central Asians are now connected to Turkey and to the world in general. Expansion of commercial ties has also been made easier by the scheduling of regular Turkish Airlines flights from Istanbul and Ankara to Ashgabat, Almaty and Tashkent. Kyrgyz charter flights also operate between Turkey and Bishkek. Istanbul has become a favoured stop-over for the businessman *en route* to Central Asia. This may only compensate in part, however, for Turkey's geographical remoteness from Central Asia.

Cultural links are being reinforced through the opening of Turkish cultural centres and schools in several Central Asian states. A Kazakh-Turkish University is being

---

39. *TDN*, 20 August 1994.
40. Much of the information in this and the next paragraph was provided to the author by the Turkish Ministry of Foreign Affairs.

developed and plans are afoot to build a Kyrgyz-Turkish University. For the 1992–93 academic year the Turkish government provided each newly independent Turkic state with 2,000 scholarships to send students and pupils to universities and schools in Turkey. There was a further intake for the next academic year but because of an apparently high drop-out rate, by the summer of 1994 only 6,000 students and pupils from the Turkic states (this time excluding Azerbaijan) were still registered. In informal discussions with the author, Central Asian students have complained about the difficulties of studying and living in Turkey on a low income. For the 1994–5 academic year 40 places were reserved for Tajik students for the first time, and the four Central Asian Turkic states were allocated 240 each.

It appears here that certain ministries are pursuing policy agendas for Central Asia which are more ambitious than the Turkish Ministry of Foreign Affairs. For example, the Turkish Education Ministry is leading a project with representatives from Azerbaijan and the Central Asian Turkic republics to prepare standard history textbooks to be introduced in schools in the 1995–6 academic year. Standard literature textbooks will follow later.[41] Working with their Central Asian counterparts, the Turkish Cultural Ministry is spearheading the work of the Turkic Cultures and Arts Joint Administration (TÜRKSOY). It is highly probable that Türkeş's National Action Party, the more extreme nationalist Great Union Party of Muhsin Yazicioğlu, the ultra-nationalist 'Turkish Clubs' Association, and other bodies based in Turkey, such as the Turkish Cultural Research Association and the Research Foundation of the Turkish World, are supporting these initiatives, which could be employed to promote the idea of cultural Pan-Turkism.

In order to familiarize the Central Asians with Turkey and the Turkish language (the Kazakh, Uzbek and Kyrgyz languages are much less closely related to modern Turkish than are Turkmen or Azeri), the Avrasya television channel has been beamed to the region since May 1992. Programmes are broadcast in Turkish with Turkish subtitles. After an agreement was made with the visiting Turkmen President in July 1994, all of the Turkic states are now able to receive Avrasya. There are differences in the length of broadcast and reception, and in some instances only the large cities are able to pick up the channel. Financial and technical difficulties, the limitation in the number of channels that are capable of being broadcast and other problems have hindered transmissions, although the quality of reception has evidently improved after TÜRKSAT 2 became operational. Rumour has it, though, that Avrasya is not particularly popular, perhaps in part because of the quality of the programmes and/or because people still do not feel comfortable with the Turkish language.

41. *Cumhuriyet*, 13 December 1994.

26

Diplomats, police officers and security personnel from the Turkic states have attended courses of instruction in Turkey. All these states have concluded military cooperation agreements which have enabled them to send small numbers of cadets to Turkey's military academies. In March 1993 the then Turkish Chief of General Staff, Doğan Güreş, even toured Central Asia. Turkey has yet to export arms to the region, but perhaps this may be possible in the longer term when the Turkic states, as Partners for Peace with NATO, may seek to standardize their inventories with the Western alliance.

It would seem that for the foreseeable future Turkey will not challenge the entrenched Russian presence in the officer corps of the Central Asian armed forces. Most officers still receive their training in Moscow. However, military cooperation in any form between Turkey and the former Soviet Central Asian republics is a sensitive issue for Moscow. For example, when in August 1994 the Turkish Defence Minister visited Kazakhstan to conclude a defence agreement, his Kazakh counterpart was at pains to emphasize that the agreement was only a 'preliminary' one dealing with cooperation in arms production and that it did not contradict the military cooperation agreements that Kazakhstan had previously concluded with other states including Russia.[42]

Although Turkey is officially a secular state, the Turkish government has also approved of cooperation with the Turkic states in the field of religion. Materials and equipment have been despatched to the region and religious education is offered for Central Asians in Turkey. It would seem that Turkish officials are at least prepared to challenge the brands of Islam which some groups from Iran and Saudi Arabia seem eager to propagate. Although information is difficult to obtain, one should note in passing here the likelihood that various 'unofficial' Islamic Sufic orders or *tariqats* operating in Turkey are also active in Central Asia. For instance, apparently Fethullah Gülen, the leader of the 'semi-illegal' Nurcu sect – which has links with the Naqshbandiyya order – has established private religious schools in Uzbekistan and elsewhere in the region in the past two years.[43] These sects are not necessarily associated with the religious Welfare Party in Turkey. Significantly, however, the newspaper *Zaman*, which does have connections with the Welfare Party (although it is not the party's official organ), appears to be the only Turkish newspaper which is widely circulated throughout Central Asia. Branch offices have been set up in Kazakhstan, Uzbekistan, Kyrgyzstan and Turkmenistan and also interestingly in the Russian republics of Tatarstan and Bashkortostan, where there are large numbers of Turkic peoples.

42. *Radio Free Europe (RFE) Daily Report*, no. 150, 9 August 1994.
43. Information obtained from Turkish academics and journalists.

Self-interest and sentiment may explain the nature and scope of Turkish involvement in Central Asia since December 1991, but the meeting of the first General Assembly of the Turkic States and Turkic Peoples' Friendship and Cooperation Group in Antalya in March 1993 was one in which the supposed close bonds of Turkic solidarity were boldly advertised. This semi-official body included popular representatives from many Turkic peoples including those from within the Russian Federation. Significantly, both President Özal and Prime Minister Demirel attended, although Türkeş appeared to orchestrate most of the proceedings. In drawing up the Declaration at the end of the gathering, the delegates appeared to be seeking to put behind them the disappointment of the first Turkic Summit. In addition to emphasizing the need to meet annually to expand cooperation in the fields of science, technology, education and culture, the Declaration referred to the prospects of developing interparliamentary cooperation and picked up the earlier proposal of Türkeş for the establishment of a High Council of Turkic Republics.[44] The slogan of the assembly – 'Dilde, fikirde, işte birlik' ('Unity in language, thought and action') – was that of one of the most renowned Pan-Turkic thinkers, Ismail Gasparali. There were thus certain groups in Turkey which, without incurring the disapproval of the government in Ankara, were aiming to create a form of Turkic Union or Commonwealth.

The second Turkic Summit

A second Turkic Summit was initially rescheduled to meet in January 1994 in Baku but was then postponed again indefinitely. It seems that the death of Özal and the domestic upheaval that ensued had diverted the attention of decision-makers in Ankara and thus perhaps less attention was given to mobilizing the Turkic leaders to attend a second summit. In the face of Russian opposition to such a meeting mobilization was indeed required. It seems that at the CIS Summit in Ashgabat in December 1993 Yeltsin had successfully pressured Karimov to lobby for the cancellation of the rescheduled Baku Summit.[45] Certainly, only two days before the leaders were to assemble the meeting was again postponed and the weaknesses of Turkic solidarity were further exposed. The Central Asian Turkic states were apparently also reluctant to meet in Baku through concern that this could send the wrong signals to Armenia. Azerbaijani officials were evidently annoyed that no Central Asian leader had yet visited Baku. Turkmenistan's supply of natural gas to Armenia also aroused resentment.

44. The text of the Declaration was provided by the Turkish Ministry of Foreign Affairs.
45. *Milliyet* (in Turkish), 27 January 1994.

Much diplomatic legwork was required before the Turkish authorities were able eventually to organize a second Turkic Summit in Istanbul in October 1994. President Demirel convinced both Niyazov and Karimov while they were in Ankara that summer to agree to Turkey hosting future Turkic summits until the meetings were regularized.[46] A definite date for the next summit was fixed only after a visit to Kazakhstan and Kyrgyzstan at the end of August by the Speaker of the Turkish Grand National Assembly, Hüsamettin Cindoruk. This was an important but controversial visit since Cindoruk as a consequence failed to attend the official opening of the Turkish parliament.

Moscow was highly critical of the summit. The spokesman of the Russian Ministry of Foreign Affairs, Mikhail Demurin, noted: 'It is unthinkable that a summit based on the principle of nationality will not disturb Russia.' He added that states grouping together on the basis of nationality 'disturb neighbouring states', and that nationalism had also led to regional tensions within the borders of the CIS. The Turkic Peoples' Assembly in Antalya was cited as an earlier example of aggressive nationalism on display.[47] Demirel retorted that the summit was neither Pan-Turkic nor directed against any state. The Turkish President also declared that, as independent countries, the Turkic states could attend such meetings if they wished without needing prior outside approval.[48] Niyazov appeared eager to alleviate Moscow's concerns by stating that cooperation among the Turkic states did not mean that responsibilities to the CIS had been forgotten.[49]

Turkish officials were probably satisfied with the results of the second Turkic Summit.[50] In contrast to the first summit, this time much less was expected. In order to avoid another disappointment, the text of the intended final document, the Istanbul Declaration, was circulated beforehand to allow participating states to consider its provisions. Nagorno-Karabakh was now mentioned: the Declaration stressed that the relevant UN Security Council resolutions concerning the Azerbaijani-Armenian conflict should be implemented. This must have pleased the Azerbaijani delegation as the resolutions underlined the need to respect the territorial integrity of Azerbaijan. The Declaration was also more specific on the issue of oil and natural gas pipelines. An article noted that oil and gas ought to be exploited and transported to the world via the most economic route and in the shortest time, and in this connection 'welcomed the work being carried out among interested countries on natural gas and oil pipelines to be

46. *Turkish Probe*, no. 83, 24 June 1994, p. 11.
47. *TDN* and *Hürriyet*, 19 October 1994.
48. *TDN*, 20 October 1994.
49. *Cumhuriyet*, 20 October 1994.
50. For the unofficial text in English of the Istanbul Declaration released at the end of the second Turkic Summit, see *TDN*, 22 October 1994.

built extending to Europe and the Mediterranean via Turkey'. The regular meetings of ministers of culture and education were praised and encouragement was given to develop further interparliamentary cooperation. A decision was also reached to hold regular meetings of foreign ministers. Finally, it was announced that the next summit would convene in Bishkek (surprisingly, in view of the earlier problems with a non-Turkish venue) in August 1995.

Although the formation of a Turkic Union or Commonwealth is not an official objective of the current Çiller government, the results of the second Turkic Summit would seem to indicate that the relations between the Turkic states – the 'Six', as some commentators in Turkey already refer to them – are becoming increasingly formalized and institutionalized. Significantly, immediately before the summit, Cindoruk had proposed in talks with Nazarbaev that the Turkic states could act together, citing the Black Sea Economic Cooperation organization as an example.[51] This organization, of which Russia is a key member, is aimed primarily at promoting the free movement of capital, goods and business entrepreneurs across the Black Sea region, and is not based on common ethnic links. A Turkic Cooperation Scheme excluding Russia would be bound to alarm Moscow, which would most probably attempt to block such a process. The Iranians and Pakistanis would also be disturbed as it would seriously challenge and put into question the continued relevance of ECO.

However, the limits of Turkic solidarity were still apparent at the second Turkic Summit. It seems that Turkey and Azerbaijan had been pressing for a much stronger wording in the final Declaration, which would have condemned the Armenian occupation of Azerbaijan. Nazarbaev apparently opposed the wording of an item labelling Armenia as an aggressor. President Heydar Aliyev of Azerbaijan evidently complained that relations between the Central Asians and Azerbaijan were not at the desired level. The Kazakh and Turkmen leaders, in the light of the recent deal between Azerbaijan and an international oil consortium on offshore oil exploration in the Caspian Sea, adopted a stance in line with Russian criticisms of the deal at that time. They declared that before the conclusion of such deals all the littoral states should first draw up an accord concerning the use of the resources of the Caspian Sea.[52]

Immediately after this event the Second General Assembly of Turkic Peoples was held in Izmir.[53] The organizers of the Izmir gathering were keen to give the impression that the Assembly was closely connected with the Turkic Summit. Again, the Turkish

51. *Hürriyet*, 18 October 1994.
52. *Turkish Probe*, no. 100, 21 October 1994.
53. For reports of the meeting, see *Sabah* (in Turkish), 19 October 1994; *Cumhuriyet*, 21 October 1994; and *TDN*, 21 and 25 October 1994. For the text of the Declaration released at the end of the meeting, see *Türk Kültürü*, Year 32, no. 380 (December 1994), pp. 711–12.

President and Prime Minister were honoured guests and participants. In her speech Çiller referred to the EU and the North American Free Trade Agreement (NAFTA) and suggested that a similar form of cooperation was possible among the Turkic states. Demirel, referring to the emergence of a Turkish/Turkic world in the past five years, noted that the members of this world were not searching for an identity because they had never lost their identity. An official at the Turkish Ministry of Foreign affairs has informed the author of this study that the Ministry was in no way connected with the work of the General Assembly. Nevertheless, the activities of this body, and the presence of leading Turkish officials at its meetings, may lead outside observers to raise questions. It is not surprising that forms of Pan-Turkic sentiment are allowed to be expressed. However, what is more intriguing is that the Turkish head of state and government deem it necessary to attend such gatherings. Sentiment would appear to remain in the foreground with regard to Turkey's interest and involvement in post-Soviet Central Asia.

6 ECONOMIC INTERESTS

Just as sentiment and self-interest are not mutually exclusive, likewise there are close connections between political and economic influence and aid and trade with regard to Turkey's relations with post-Soviet Central Asia. It appears that Turkish officials and businessmen underestimated the amount of aid and capital the Central Asians required and failed to realize fully the scale of the economic difficulties confronting the newly independent Turkic states. The extent of economic and hence political dependence of the former Soviet Central Asians on Moscow was also not fully appreciated at first. Without mentioning specifics, Umut Arık, the TIKA Chairman, noted how Turkey initially had made unrealistic promises and proposals by offering up to $3 billion in support to the Turkic states. Turkey had wanted to be the principal supplier of aid but this was clearly beyond its capacity. The vast size and great potential in the Central Asian region meant that it was neither economically feasible nor politically possible for Turkey alone to develop the market there.[54] More hard-headed realism soon emerged, although not at the expense of sentiment. Turkey has been reasonably generous in its granting of humanitarian assistance and allocation of credits, but Turkish business has also become actively involved in the region in the search for profits.

The Turkish authorities have often drawn attention to the relevance of the application of the so-called Turkish economic model for the Central Asians. One common argument is that Turkey's recent experience of economic reform after 1980, when the structure of a market economy was set in place, could be emulated by the Turkic states. Officials in Turkey are also keen to stress that Turkish companies can be important partners for Western firms which are seeking business opportunities in Central Asia.

In practice, the familiarity of Turkish entrepreneurs with the culture of the region and the closeness of the language – important especially for social purposes – does enable the Turks to adapt more readily than Western business people to local conditions in Central Asia.[55] Americans and West Europeans often experience difficulties in

54. *TDN*, 20 August 1994.
55. Information in this paragraph was obtained from a Turkish businessman active in Central Asia.

negotiating and bargaining with their prospective Central Asian clients. Smaller Turkish companies, in particular, are more willing to take risks in an unstable business environment where proper tax regulations and legal frameworks are lacking, whereas some larger Turkish companies are loath to invest in the region because of the absence of an effective infrastructure. Cooperation between Turkish and Western companies can be mutually beneficial, with the latter providing much-needed capital and more sophisticated technology, and Turkish companies providing quality labour at a reasonable cost. Several multinational corporations (MNCs) eager to link up with Central Asia have found it useful to establish a base in Turkey, since they can then employ less expensive Turkish sub-contractors and personnel to secure access to Central Asia. However, more recently Western companies have begun to prefer to operate in the region through Moscow rather than via Istanbul and Ankara in order to tap the larger Russian market as well.

The financial collapse within Turkey since January 1994 must have discouraged Turkish entrepreneurs from taking risks in what is still an insecure market. The Turkish economy has suffered a serious decline in industrial production after the sharp devaluation of the Turkish lira against the dollar followed by the imposition of harsh austerity measures in April 1994. The perennial problems of a high rate of inflation (over 150% according to some reports in February 1995) and a huge budget deficit remain to be tackled. Ironically, one possible remedy is the privatization of inefficient state economic enterprises which were not affected by the major structural reforms of the early 1980s. Given these difficulties and shortcomings, doubts must be raised about the appropriateness of the Turkish economic model for the Turkic states.

The problems in the Central Asian economies are immense. Only Tajikistan has opted to enter the new rouble zone at the price of becoming totally economically dependent on Moscow. The other Central Asian states, refusing to accept the stringent conditions imposed by Russia for entry to the new zone, are thus no longer able to benefit from Moscow's subsidies. The Turkic states are desperately in need of foreign capital and new technology to diversify their economies. Under Soviet rule the Central Asians had basically supplied Moscow with raw materials, particularly cotton. In the transition from a command to a market economy major structural reforms must be undertaken, and at the same time new road and rail networks and oil and gas pipelines need to be constructed to enable the region to become more economically independent of Moscow. In the short to medium term the economic situation will remain critical. Throughout the area output is falling, budget deficits are mushrooming, and unemployment and inflation are increasing. In some instances there are serious food shortages. This is potentially very destabilizing given that the civil strife of the late 1980s in the region was largely the result of a shortage of jobs. The situation may only improve in the longer term if increased outside investment enables the Central Asians to extract and deliver their oil, gas, minerals, other raw materials and processed goods to the outside world and thereby generate hard-currency earnings.

Before examining the nature and extent of Turkey's aid and credit programmes in Central Asia, it is important to note in passing the size of investments, loans etc. provided by the international community in order to put them in perspective.[56] For instance, Chevron has pledged a total of $20 billion over the next 40 years to develop the huge Tengiz oilfield in Kazakhstan. British Gas and Agip have offered to invest $6 billion to develop Kazakhstan's Karachaganak natural gas field. The IMF has developed a programme to salvage the Kyrgyz economy but this will require an infusion of at least $400 million. Until recently Turkmenistan and Uzbekistan received little international credit as a result of their failure to present real reform programmes. Early Turkish offers of aid and credit must have been appreciated in these instances, although large companies are now making substantial investments in Uzbekistan in particular. For example, British American Tobacco is reportedly investing $140–150 million to modernize and build tobacco factories in Uzbekistan. According to a senior World Bank official, Uzbekistan requires $5 billion in loans over the next five years for investment in strategic sectors of the economy.

Turkish aid and credit programmes

By the end of 1994 Turkey had extended over $78 million of humanitarian aid to the five post-Soviet Central Asian states.[57] Uzbekistan was by far the largest beneficiary, receiving $54 million; Tajikistan received only $404,000. Credits have also been extended to Kyrgyzstan and Uzbekistan for the purchase of food. By December 1994 over 24,000 tonnes of wheat valued at $2.6 million had been shipped to Kyrgyzstan from Turkey using this credit facility. In the case of Uzbekistan, 624,000 tonnes of wheat worth $8.3 million and over 216,000 tonnes of sugar valued at over $62 million had been delivered by Turkey.

As Table 1 shows, the Turkish Eximbank has opened a number of credit lines to assist Turkey's export drive to Central Asia. Credits, which should eventually be paid back, have been offered to enable the hard-currency-starved Central Asians to procure Turkish foodstuffs and goods, and to finance the work of Turkish construction projects in the region. Apparently, the cost of Turkish construction work in Central Asia amounts

56. Details in this paragraph are from various issues in 1993 and 1994 of the *Country Report – Georgia, Armenia, Azerbaijan, Kazakhstan, Central Asian Republics* (hereafter cited as *Country Report*), London, Economist Intelligence Unit.
57. Information in this paragraph was provided to the author by the Turkish Ministry of Foreign Affairs.

Table 1 Turkish Eximbank credits to Post-Soviet Central Asia ($ million)

	Total credit limit			Credit for projects			Credit for goods and foodstuffs		
	Total	Amount credit opened	Amount credit used	Total	Amount credit opened	Amount credit used	Total	Amount credit opened	Amount credit used
Uzbekistan	250	177.63	141.98	125	52.63	17.40	125	125	124.58
Kazakhstan	200	141.56	86.61	144.3	97.41	46.72	55.7	44.15	39.89
Turkmenistan	91	93.15	85.48	16	14.20	10.49	75	78.95	74.99
Kyrgyzstan	75	70.09	25.63	46.28	39.95	4.80	28.72	30.14	20.83
Tajikistan	50	17.12	16.06				50	17.12	16.06
Total	666	499.55	355.76	331.58	204.19	79.41	334.42	295.36	276.35

Source: Turkish Eximbank. Figures good as of 15 November 1994.

to around $3.7 billion and is thus only exceeded by similar work undertaken by Turkish contractors in Libya and Russia. Immediately before the second Turkic Summit Nazarbaev and Akayev requested from Demirel additional credits of $300 million and $25 million respectively.[58]

A portion of the Turkish Eximbank credits which were initially agreed upon with the Central Asian states and offered on very favourable terms have yet to be opened, and credits when opened have not been fully used. Only a little over half of the total credit limit agreed upon with these states has actually been utilized. In particular, credits allocated for use in certain projects appear to have run into difficulties. The procedures for the opening and use of credits are complicated and cumbersome, and evidently the Central Asians themselves are often unsure which projects should be financed.[59] There are also doubts about whether Turkey is in a position to raise all the promised funds given the current situation of the Turkish economy. This has not deterred the Central Asian leaders from requesting additional credit support. Repayment will also not be easy given the difficulties Turkey has already encountered with Moscow with regard to the extension of Turkish Eximbank credits. Interestingly, in March 1994 the General Manager of the Turkish Eximbank, Ahmet Ertuğrul, announced the first co-financing venture between the Eximbanks of Turkey and Japan, where a loan of $200 million was agreed upon to assist a Turkish firm construct an iron and steel factory in Kazakhstan.[60] The Turkish Eximbank may conclude other such co-financing ventures

58. *TDN* and *Cumhuriyet*, 18 October 1994.
59. Interview with Nihat Gökyiğit, Chairman of the Turkey-CIS Business Council, Istanbul, 20 October 1994.
60. *Cumhuriyet*, 17 March 1994.

in the future. There are also apparently plans to allow the Turkish Eximbank to concentrate more on funding a country risk insurance scheme. Another problem with the Turkish Eximbank scheme is that credits are only offered on a short-term basis. For medium-term financing, other arrangements are needed.

Trade

Trade turnover between Turkey and post-Soviet Central Asia has risen in volume from just over $145 million in 1992 to $550 million in 1993 (see Table 2). These figures amounted to 7.5% and 16.5% of Turkey's total trade with all of the former Soviet republics in 1992 and 1993 respectively. Among the Central Asians Uzbekistan is clearly the most important trade partner for Turkey, but in 1993 Russia still accounted for over 60% of the Turkey's trade turnover with all of the former Soviet republics. One should also bear in mind that the share of Turkey's trade with Central Asia as a percentage of Turkey's total trade turnover is very small. For instance, in 1992 and 1993 Turkey's exports to Uzbekistan were 0.4% and 1.4% of its total exports in those years.[61] According to one prominent Turkish businessman, Turkey is currently importing more than is necessary from the Central Asians in order to boost their economies by paying for these imports in hard currency.[62] The low levels of bilateral trade between Turkey and the Central Asian states are explained in part by the fact that Turkey preferred to participate in construction projects in the region, as noted above. In order to boost trade turnover there would have to be an improvement in distribution channels, financing, credit and banking services. The goods would also have to be transported more efficiently. At present, Turkish lorry drivers often experience difficulties in carrying their freight to Central Asia through an overland route via Iran. A railway line connecting Turkey and Central Asia has yet to be completed, and in any case a stretch of this will also pass through Iran. The distance between Turkey and Central Asia and the problem of access pose more severe logistical problems for Turkish businesses than for, say, their Iranian competitors.

In 1993, 54.59%, 49.78%, 40.76% and 27.49% of Turkish exports to Turkmenistan, Kyrgyzstan, Kazakhstan and Uzbekistan respectively consisted of machinery and transport equipment. Food accounted for 56.16% and 20.8% of Turkish exports to Uzbekistan and Turkmenistan respectively. Textiles and clothing were also important items exported to Kazakhstan and Kyrgyzstan. Agricultural raw materials made up 91.79%, 88.41%, 33.44% and just over 20% of Turkish imports from Turkmenistan,

61. For these figures see *Turkish Probe*, no. 102, 4 November 1994, p. 25.
62. Interview with Nihat Gökyiğit, Chairman of the Turkey-CIS Business Council, Istanbul, 20 October 1994.

Table 2 Trade between Turkey and Russia and former Soviet Central Asia in 1992 and 1993 ($ '000)

	1992						1993					
	Exports		Imports		Trade turnover		Exports		Imports		Trade turnover	
	Amount	%	Amount	%	Amount	%	Amount	%	Amount	%	Amount	%
Total for Former Soviet Union	685,743	100.0	1,244,448	100.0	1,930,191	100.0	1,047,119	100.0	2,284,518	100.0	3,331,637	100.0
Russian Federation	441,997	64.5	1,040,577	83.6	1,482,574	76.81	504,597	48.2	1,542,330	67.5	2,046,927	61.44
Uzbekistan	54,492	7.9	21,019	1.7	75,511	3.91	213,501	20.4	31,925	1.4	245,426	7.36
Kazakhstan	19,379	2.8	10,511	0.8	29,890	1.55	67,801	6.5	43,741	1.9	111,542	3.35
Turkmenistan	7,495	1.1	21,181	1.7	28,676	1.49	83,886	8.0	76,892	3.4	160,778	4.82
Tajikistan	706	0.1	7,762	0.6	8,468	0.44	4,805	0.5	6,796	0.3	11,601	0.35
Kyrgyzstan	1,831	0.3	1,442	0.1	3,273	0.17	17,044	1.6	3,470	0.2	20,514	0.62

Sources: For 1992, *Şubat 1993'de Türkiye Ekonomisi İstatistik ve Yorumlar (The Turkish Economy in February 1993, Statistics and Comments)*, Ankara, T C Başbakanlık Devlet İstatistik Enstitüsü, February 1993, Table 28 in the Foreign Trade Section. For 1993, *Nisan 1994'te Türkiye Ekonomisi İstatistik ve Yorumlar (The Turkish Economy in April 1994, Statistics and Comments)*, Ankara, T C Başbakanlık Devlet İstatistik Enstitüsü, April 1994, Tables 16 and 17 in the Foreign Trade Section. Trade turnover figures were not originally included.

Uzbekistan, Kyrgyzstan and Kazakhstan respectively. Almost 50% of Turkish imports from Kyrgyzstan consisted of food and over 61% of imports from Kazakhstan were of iron, steel and non-ferrous metals.[63] These figures reveal the import needs of the Central Asians at present, as well as indicating the more developed and diversified nature of the Kazakh economy. In the longer term, if the Turkic states are able to extract and transport large quantities of oil and natural gas, the percentage of Turkish imports of agricultural raw materials in the commodity composition of trade would most probably be considerably reduced.

Official trade figures do not necessarily give the full picture. Although it is not possible to quantify exactly, there does appear to be some exchange of goods between Turkey and Central Asia using the grey/black market. However, the transportation problems noted above and the distances involved would seem to indicate that the extent of this 'unofficial' trade is probably relatively small.

Investment and joint ventures

To promote and further develop official commercial ties, business councils have been established between Turkey and all the newly independent states of post-Soviet Central Asia. The Turkish-Uzbek business council was formed as early as November 1991. Turkey is also actively involved in the field of banking, providing training programmes and offering technical expertise. For example, the state Ziraat (Agricultural) Bank has concluded joint venture agreements with banks in Kazakhstan, Uzbekistan and Turkmenistan. Although short of capital to finance large-scale construction projects, Turkey is nevertheless involved in supporting the building of hotels, textile and cement factories, copper cable production plants, etc. through the use of Turkish Eximbank credits and deals struck by Turkish firms with still largely government-state companies in Central Asia. Thus Turkey is usefully contributing to the development of small-scale industrialization in the region, especially in the processing sector. Previously, cotton grown in Central Asia had to be transported westward for processing in other parts of the Soviet Union.

As of June 1994, 22 Turkish-Kyrgyz joint ventures were operational, mostly in mining, telecommunications, leather, food, tourism, foreign trade and construction.[64]

63. These figures are from Subidey Toğan, 'Black Sea Economic Cooperation, Economic Cooperation Organization, Turkic Republics and Turkey, possibilities for regional economic cooperation', Paper presented at the Conference on 'European Union-Turkey-Eurasia: New Trends in EU-Turkey Cooperation', organized by the European Community Institute of Marmara University, Istanbul, and the Trans-European Policy Studies Association (TEPSA), 22–23 September 1994, Istanbul.
64. Unless otherwise stated in this and in the following paragraphs information is from the country reports of the *DEIK Bulletin* (Foreign Economic Relations Board, Istanbul), June 1994 issues.

This was in contrast to 64 Chinese-Krygyz registered joint ventures. One of the largest joint ventures signed between Turkey and Kyrgyzstan in 1992 made the company BMB (Birleşmiş Mühendisler Bürosu) responsible for the operation of two substantial gold fields for a period of 30 years.

With regard to Uzbekistan, 7% of all joint ventures concluded by the Uzbeks are with Turkish companies. This compares with a figure of 19% for American businesses. Turkey is particularly active in the field of textiles, hotel construction, the production of telecommunications equipment, and the building of a cement factory. In October 1994 it was reported that Turkish firms were involved in projects in Uzbekistan worth $446 million.[65]

In Turkmenistan Turkish investment amounts to $650.7 million. This covers a wide range of activities including the building of a bakery, a housing complex, flour mills, pasta plants, leather factories and help in the telecommunications field. Turkish companies are involved in 15 different projects to increase the local cotton-processing capacity. In the autumn of 1994 almost 20,000 Turkish workers were employed in Turkmenistan on various projects.[66] Speaking in Turkmenistan in October 1994, Demirel announced that Turkish firms might invest up to $10 billion in Turkmenistan in the next ten years.[67]

There are over 100 joint ventures between Turkey and Kazakhstan, concentrated in the energy, construction, mining, maritime transportation and trading sectors. As of August 1994 Turkish firms were involved in contracts worth $1.7 billion. The construction company ENTEŞ alone had won four contracts valued at $765 million to build a copper rod factory, an iron and steel works, a bank and a cable factory.[68] The energy reserves of Kazakhstan are particularly attractive, and in June 1994 Turkey and Kazakhstan agreed to develop jointly seven oil and gas fields in that country. The fields have reserves of 4 billion barrels of oil and almost 390 billion cubic metres of gas, of which Turkey will receive 211 million barrels of oil and almost 210 billion cubic metres of gas.[69] In these deals an element of risk is involved. For example, in July 1992 BMB agreed to operate four oilfields and to construct a thermal power station worth $1.7 billion in Kazakhstan; by November of that year it was reported that three of the oilfields allocated by the Kazakh government had been found to be unproductive.[70]

65. *Milliyet*, 19 October 1994.
66. *Cumhuriyet*, 25 October 1994.
67. *TDN*, 29 October 1994.
68. *Ibid.*, 24 August 1994.
69. *Country Report*, 3rd Quarter 1994, London, Economist Intelligence Unit, 1994, p. 50.
70. Robins, *op. cit.* (see note 36), p. 598.

The highly unstable situation in Tajikistan has prevented the development of commercial relations between Turkey and Tajikistan. Trade turnover figures are minimal, though Turkish officials have expressed a future interest in helping to develop Tajik aluminium production. In 1994, following an earlier agreement between the Turkish company Yazex and the Tajik government to build three cotton mills, Turkey announced that it would provide credits to help Tajikistan build, *inter alia*, twelve small cotton processing factories in northern Tajikistan.[71]

Prospects for cooperation

As noted earlier, Turkey is willing to cooperate with other interested states in expanding economic ties in post-Soviet Central Asia. This could circumvent the problem of the lack of Turkish capital. Hitherto, the record here is mixed. In 1992 the lobbying efforts of the Turkish government to encourage the West to divert more aid and investment to Central Asia rather than Russia were not successful. However, one spin-off of Demirel's visit to the United States in February 1992 was the despatch of a joint mission of the Turkish Foreign Economics Relations Board (DEIK) and the Turkish-American Businessman's Association to Central Asia in June 1992. A similar DEIK-Japanese (Keidanren) group toured the region in April 1993. The Japanese delegation suggested that its government should finance a technical cooperation centre in Turkey to support human resources development in Central Asia, but this centre is yet to be established.

Cooperation between Turkey and the United States has been more productive. Possibly the most significant deal was the public announcement in late October 1994 of a memorandum of cooperation signed by the United States, Israel and Turkey. This provided for agricultural assistance and training in Uzbekistan and Turkmenistan to establish two sample farms and agricultural development centres. Turkey will offer its know-how on open irrigation, the Israelis will supply expertise in more developed irrigation techniques, and the United States will presumably provide finance.[72]

Cooperation between Britain and Turkey in Central Asia has not fully taken off. It appears that several British companies prefer to operate in Central Asia from branches in Moscow rather than in Istanbul or Ankara. One of the most successful ventures has been the partnership between the construction companies Alarko and John Laing to build a new terminal at Ashgabat airport valued at $54 million, which Demirel officially opened in October 1994. This has been a classic example of the marriage of Western capital and Turkish manpower.

71. *Country Report*, 3rd Quarter 1994, London, Economist Intelligence Unit, p. 64.
72. *TDN*, 1 November 1994.

The EU is clearly aware of the value of using Turkish expertise and familiarity with the region to contribute towards its own aid programme for Central Asia. However, there has been a long internal debate within the EU over whether some TACIS (Technical Assistance to the CIS) funds should be used to pay for direct Turkish participation in assisting the Turkic states.[73] It remains to be seen, moreover, how Turkey's economic relations with Central Asia will be affected if Turkey is able to enter the EU Customs Union by the end of 1995. One of the objectives of the original members of ECO – Turkey, Iran and Pakistan – was to create a customs union, although the organization's new members – the newly independent Central Asian states, Azerbaijan and Afghanistan – have yet to commit themselves to the same goal. It is possible in theory for Turkey to be simultaneously a member of two customs unions. Membership of the EU Customs Union, for example, would merely involve the elimination of quotas, tariffs and the reduction of tax rates without adopting the common external tax rate of the EU.

73. Robins, *op. cit.* (see note 36), p. 602.

7 COMPETITION AND COOPERATION? TURKEY, RUSSIA AND IRAN

Pakistan and Iran, together with Russia and in the longer term China, are all to some extent economic and political rivals of Turkey in Central Asia. This section focuses, in particular, on how Turkish officials perceive Iran and Russia as competitors or cooperation partners in the region. As the Soviet Union was collapsing, many commentators speculated that a new Great Game for influence in Central Asia might unfold, reminiscent of the one played out between Britain and Russia in the nineteenth century. This time most agreed that the key actors were Turkey, Iran and Russia, although Pakistan, India, Israel and Saudi Arabia have also been referred to as interested players, and it is suggested that China could eventually become an even more serious competitor. After a period of cosying up to the West, by mid-1992 the Yeltsin administration was gradually assuming more interest in the 'near abroad'. This was in part due to concern for the fate of the substantial Russian minorities still resident in the former Soviet republics, and, with particular reference to the Caucasus and Central Asia, out of a fear that radicalized and politicized Islam could spread in the near abroad and from there have an impact on the large Muslim population in the Russian Federation. Russian nationalists also began to argue more persuasively that the establishment of close control over the members of the CIS was a matter of prestige. One analyst has referred to various permutations in the competition for influence in Central Asia. Russia and Iran might cooperate together against Turkey; Iran and Turkey might combine in opposition to Russia; and Russia and Turkey might coordinate their activities to check Iran. It was suggested that the first combination was most probable because of the likelihood of the formation of a Turkey-US-Israel axis, taking into account Turkey's enhanced interest in Mediterranean security and Çiller's landmark visit to Israel in the autumn of 1994.[74] In practice, however, the Turkish authorities have perceived neither Iran nor Russia as outright competitors for influence in Central Asia.

74. 'Turkey and Iran', Paper presented by Henri Barkey at the 26th National Convention of the American Association for the Advancement of Slavic Studies (AAASS), 19 November 1994, Philadelphia.

Russia

The Yeltsin administration seems to have deliberately exaggerated to some extent its fears of the revival of Pan-Turkism in order to steal the thunder of the Russian extreme nationalist right. Stalin's anxieties with regard to the possible emergence of a Pan-Turkic movement have not been forgotten in Russia. However, an element of Turcophobia may also be influencing decision-makers in Moscow. Zhirinovsky's hostile rantings against Turkey and his dream of conquering 'Constantinople' are well-known. But more serious analysts such as Alexei Arbatov, the Head of the Department of the Institute of World Economy and International Relations of the Russian Academy of Sciences, have also pointed to a potential Turkish threat. Arguing that Turkey should be prevented from having direct communication with the Turkic peoples of Central Asia through Azerbaijan and the South Caspian area, Arbatov also reiterated what is becoming a commonly expressed Russian fear of Tatarstan and Bashkortostan coming under the influence of Islamic fundamentalism and separatism (the latter most probably inspired by Turkey because of the Turkic connection), which could split Russia in two along the Volga.[75]

The Russian authorities were clearly annoyed at what seems to have been an off-the-cuff remark by Demirel in April 1992, suggesting that the Turkic states could not be considered fully independent as long as they remained within the rouble zone.[76] Yet Ankara appears to have acted with considerable diplomatic tact in response to Tatarstan's overtures to develop closer relations. The Turkish authorities notified Moscow in advance of the visit of Tatarstan's President Shaimiyev to Ankara in October 1992, and in July 1994 the Turkish Deputy Prime Minister Murat Karayalçin asked his visiting Russian counterpart for cooperation to allow the opening of a Turkish consulate in Kazan in the light of expanding commercial ties between Turkey and Tatarstan.[77] Ankara, apparently, has offended Russian sensitivities with regard to non-Turkic but predominantly Muslim Chechenia. The Chechen leader Dzhokhar Dudaev has visited Turkey – which has a large Chechen community – on at least two occasions, but after Demirel received Dudaev in October 1993 the Turkish ambassador in Moscow was summoned to give assurances that such a meeting would not be repeated.[78] With Moscow's armed intervention in Chechenia in December 1994, Ankara was careful not to condemn the deployment but appealed instead for a peaceful solution to the problem. However, Turkish officials

75. Alexei G. Arbatov, 'Russian Foreign Policy Priorities for the 1990s', in T.P. Johnson and S. Miller (eds), *Russian Security after the Cold War* (Wasington DC: Brasseys, 1994), pp. 26–27.
76. *Turkey Confidential*, no. 30, 1992, p. 11.
77. *RFE Daily Report*, no. 135, 19 July 1994.
78. *Balkan News* (Athens), 17 October 1993.

became more critical when the citizens of Grozny were the victims of an indiscriminate aerial and artillery bombardment.

In contrast to the case of Central Asia, Turkey's relations with Russia in connection with the Caucasus and Transcaucasia are much more problematic. Moscow's desire to revise the CFE Treaty with reference to the number of its troops and tanks allowed in the Caucasus, its meddling in Georgia and Azerbaijan, and its reluctance to allow a genuine international peacekeeping force in Nagorno-Karabakh have all met fierce criticism in Ankara because of the perceived threat to Turkey's security. Central Asia, on the other hand, is not strategically crucial for Turkey. Many Turkish officials are aware that the Central Asian leaderships benefited from the former Soviet regime and that they still wish to remain part of a Russian security umbrella. This is largely out of a concern that Islamic radicalism should not engulf the region and create a new Afghanistan-type situation. The Central Asian leaders are also keen to avoid the internal turmoil witnessed in Tajikistan. Even Turkmenistan, which was not a party to the Tashkent Collective Security Agreement, has concluded bilateral defence agreements with Russia to permit the stationing of thousands of Russian troops along the Turkmen–Iranian border. With the exception of Kyrgyzstan, the post-Soviet Central Asian states would have wished to remain in the old rouble zone.

Economic support from Turkey and the development of close cultural ties between Turkey and the Turkic states could help to foster stability in the Central Asian region and would thus be appreciated by Moscow. However, in order to avoid tensions with Moscow Ankara should keep its Pan-Turkic supporters in check, and Turkish officials should not be seen to be openly espousing goals such as the creation of a Turkic Union or Confederation. Relations between Turkey and Russia in general have continued to improve in recent years. Trade turnover is considerably higher than between Turkey and the former Central Asian republics. In May 1992 Demirel signed a Friendship and Cooperation Agreement in Moscow. Çiller concluded another important visit to Moscow in September 1993. Both Turkey and Russia are key members of the Black Sea Economic Cooperation organization. Relations could, however, deteriorate if Yeltsin were voted out of office and replaced by a more hardline nationalist figure.

The pipelines question

The problems in relations between Azerbaijan and the other Turkic states illustrate the fact that Central Asia and Transcaucasia cannot be rigidly separated. In the case of Russia and Turkey the pipelines issue is a common factor and a source of tension and rivalry. Until recently, Moscow was determined to ensure that the Central Asians and Azerbaijanis remained to some extent economically and hence politically dependent on Russia by insisting that the pipelines which transported oil from these states continued to flow through Russia. Thus many Russian officials were highly critical of the deal signed on 20 September 1994 between an international oil consortium and the Azerbaijani authorities to explore and develop oil in the Caspian Sea. This oil could possibly be transported via Azerbaijan and Iran, or through Armenia and Nakhichevan, or across Georgia to the Turkish Mediterranean coast at Ceyhan before then being shipped to its final destination. Additional pipelines carrying oil from Kazakhstan and Turkmenistan could also be connected to one of these routes. Moscow opposed the scheme in spite of the fact that a Russian company, LUKoil, has a 10% stake in the deal. This compares with the meagre 1.75% stake originally offered to the Turkish State Petroleum Agency (although in early February 1995 Turkish officials had secured an agreement in principle to raise the Agency's share to 6.75%).

At present oil extracted in Azerbaijan is transported by railway to Novorossiisk or Odessa or by tanker across the Caspian Sea to northern Iran. An old oil pipeline between Baku and Novorossiisk which runs through the Chechen capital, Grozny, was already out of use before the outbreak of hostilities in Chechenia in late 1994. Most Russian officials are in favour of constructing a new oil pipeline between Baku and Novorossiisk. Oil would then be transported to the Mediterranean either by tanker through the Straits or to the Bulgarian port of Burgas from where a new pipeline could be built to the Greek port of Alexandroupolis. The oil could then be shipped from Greece, thus avoiding further congestion of the Straits which could pose an environmental threat to Istanbul, and at the same time bypassing Turkey. Moscow is also in favour of transporting oil from Kazakhstan and Turkmenistan through the old system of Soviet pipelines.

By early February 1995, however, Russian officials were becoming resigned to the likelihood of an oil pipeline from Baku to Ceyhan via Armenia and Nakhichevan (if a lasting peace settlement could be achieved over Nagorno-Karabakh) or through Georgia. The US administration announced support for a Baku-Ceyhan oil pipeline. Long-standing American hostility to Iran appears to eliminate any early prospects for a pipeline through Iran. Ironically, it appears that Iran's interest in participating in the international oil consortium – though that participation remains uncertain after a meeting of the consortium in London in February 1995 – isolated those in Moscow who were opposed to the September 1994 oil deal. The probability of continued unrest in Chechenia, the limited loading capacity of Novorossiisk, and the argument made by Turkish officials that the Baku-Ceyhan route would only be an alternative to a Baku-Novorossiisk route and was not intended to siphon off all the oil Azerbaijan produced, were other factors that may have swayed Russian officials. The authorities in Ankara are also hoping that Kazakh oil from Tengiz could link up with the Baku-Ceyhan route through the construction of connecting pipelines. In spite of earlier support from the US administration and Chevron for the construction of a new oil pipeline from the Tengiz oil field to Novorossiisk – agreed upon by the Caspian Pipeline Consortium of Russia, Oman,

Kazakhstan and Chevron – the United States might also support work on another pipeline connecting Tengiz to Baku. This could perhaps be in reaction to the violent Russian repression of the Chechen separatists – although the Caspian Pipeline Consortium has also run into difficulties over financing. In early February 1995 the Russian Oil and Energy Minister Yuri Shafranik declared that provided Russia could use its pipelines to carry its share of oil from Azerbaijan and Kazakhstan to southern Russia, the Azeris and Kazakhs would then be free to use whatever route they wished to transport the remainder of their oil.[79]

However, Russia appears to be cooperating with both Turkey and Iran in a project to construct a natural gas pipeline from Turkmenistan to Central Europe via Iran and Turkey. The heads of state of Turkey, Pakistan, Azerbaijan and Iran and the Russian Foreign Minister Andrei Kozyrev were in Ashgabat to celebrate the symbolic inauguration of the project in October 1994. Representatives from Turkey, Russia, Iran, Kazakhstan and Turkmenistan sit in a number of steering committees which have been set up to realize the project, and each state has pledged to assist in financing it. Why should Russia be supporting Turkmenistan's efforts to open a new gas pipeline in order to provide an alternative to the sole pipeline currently running north through Russia? Does this stem from a calculation on Moscow's part that the project will never be realized because of Western reluctance to offer money for a pipeline that would cross Iran? It does seem likely that in the long term only a Turkmen-Iranian-Turkish natural gas pipeline will be built. Without Western financial backing it will not be possible to construct a gas pipeline all the way to Vienna. Niyazov's visit to Turkey in January 1995 to promote the project failed to secure pledges of outside financial assistance. There is a definite need for Turkey to diversify its imports of natural gas. The Turkish consumer has become too dependent on Russian natural gas, which is at times illegally siphoned off *en route* to Turkey by an energy-starved and debt-ridden Ukraine.

Iran

Secular Turkey and revolutionary Iran are ideological rivals in the sense that both are Muslim countries which offer alternative models of political development. However, Tehran does not appear to be consciously seeking to impose its form of politicized religious radicalism on what is a predominantly Sunni Muslim Central Asia. In the traditionally semi-nomadic societies of Kazakhstan and Kyrgyzstan, where there are also now large Russian minorities, Islam has never been a potent political force. All the current Central Asian leaderships are very wary of the possible spread of Iranian-

79. *TDN*, 4 February 1995.

inspired religious activism in the region. Although Turkey and Iran certainly appear to be rivals in Central Asia in the cultural and economic spheres, Turkish officials have consistently denied that such a rivalry exists. When Demirel reiterated this standard line at the Ashgabat Summit of the former Soviet Central Asian Republics, Turkey, Iran and Pakistan in May 1992, Iranian President Rafsanjani stated that there was competition which should be 'honest' and 'healthy'.[80] If an open conflict were to break out between the traditionally rival Tajiks and Uzbeks, Iran and Turkey might be forced to support the Persian and Turkic camps. Ironically, the competition between Ankara and Tehran could also intensify and assume a new dimension if the religious Welfare Party were to secure power in Turkey and then seek to implement its vision of a new Islamic World centred on Turkey.

History has shown that both Turkey and Iran can lay claim to common cultural, religious and ethnic links with the various peoples of Central Asia. In spite of the presence of Persian Tajiks in Tajikistan, Uzbekistan and Afghanistan, the authorities in Tehran have not promoted a policy of radical Pan-Iranism. Such a policy would only contribute to the destabilization of the region by also encouraging the rekindling of Pan-Turkism and aggravating Iran's own large Azerbaijani and Turkmen population. Not until 1992 did Iran venture to establish a cultural association of Persian-speaking peoples in the region, comprising Iran, Tajikistan and Afghanistan.

Turkey and Iran have clashed in a struggle to establish cultural supremacy in the region in what may be referred to as the battle of the alphabets. The Central Asians were confronted with the choice of switching back from the Cyrillic script to either the Latin or the Arabic alphabet. The Latin alphabet had been employed for only a few years after the Bolshevik revolution. In promoting the Latin script Turkey was challenged not only by Iran but by the whole Arab world and the financial clout of, for instance, the Islamic Development Bank. Tajikistan was the only state which decided to revert to the Arabic alphabet. Following Azerbaijan, Uzbekistan and Turkmenistan have made firm commitments to adopt the Latin script by 1 September 1995 and 1 January 1996 respectively, although it will take several years and thousands of Turkish books and typewriters before the alphabet becomes generally familiar. Kazakhstan and Kyrgyzstan have also provisionally agreed to employ the Latin script. The fact that the Turkish language uses basically the same script as the major Western languages has helped Turkey to triumph in the battle of the alphabets.

In practice, Turkey and Iran are also competing for enhanced economic influence in the region. Both are seeking to benefit from the expanded trade, transport dues and prestige that would result if the Central Asians were to agree to the use of Turkish or

---

80. *Ibid.*, 11 May 1992.

Iranian ports and were to support the construction of roads, railways and pipelines connecting Turkey or Iran with the region. Iranian Gulf ports are much less accessible to the West than Turkey's Mediterranean facilities, and for political reasons the United States would prefer to trade with Central Asia without having Iran as a middleman. On geographic grounds, however, Iran is in a favourable position to expand commercial links with neighbouring Turkmenistan and with Kazakhstan – which, like Iran, are also Caspian Sea littoral states. Iranian expertise in the oil and gas industry could be drawn on to consolidate links with Turkmenistan. There are plans to construct an oil pipeline between Turkmenistan and Iran. Joint shipping lines and companies have been established with both Turkmenistan and Kazakhstan.

In a further attempt to exploit the Caspian Sea connection, in 1992 Iran sponsored the formation of a Caspian Sea Cooperation Scheme with Russia, Azerbaijan, Kazakhstan and Turkmenistan. At the time this looked like a response to Turkey's moves to create the Black Sea Economic Cooperation. Recently, Russia has been attempting to hijack the original Iranian project in the hope of transforming the scheme into a multilateral coordinating committee which could possibly work to apportion the resources of the Caspian Sea in a manner that is beneficial to Russia.

In spite of these elements of Turkish–Iranian competition, economic cooperation between Turkey and Iran in Central Asia is also possible. Both states are key participants in the Turkmen natural gas project. A possible new Azerbaijani oil pipeline from the Caspian Sea offshore oilfields could in theory cross both Iran and Turkey. In late November 1994 the Iranian Deputy Foreign Minister, Abbas Maleki, held talks in Ankara on oil, gas and transportation projects as a guest of TIKA.[81] Turkey and Iran are principal members of ECO, one of whose objectives is to develop a network of pipelines and power grids to meet the requirements of the Central Asians. The two states are also important trading partners and both have a common interest in resolving the Kurdish issue. Most probably, Turkish officials would want to avoid an open contest with Iran in Central Asia because of Turkey's dependence both on Iranian oil and on Tehran's continued willingness to limit its support to the guerrillas of the PKK (Kurdish Workers' Party), who are engaged in a violent struggle against the authorities in Ankara.

Other players

Pakistan and Saudi Arabia are not major players in Central Asia. Experience in banking, insurance and knowledge of English would appear to make Pakistan a possible rival for Turkey in the region. However, continued instability in Afghanistan is seriously impairing

81. *Ibid.*, 24 November 1994.

links between Central Asia and Pakistan and is preventing the use of the ports of Gwaidar and Karachi. Turkey and Pakistan have excellent relations, and both are cooperating in the Turkmen natural gas project. Pakistan has been perceived as much less of a threat to Turkey's interests in Central Asia since Islamabad apparently dropped its support of radical Islamic groups in the region. Instead, there is a tense rivalry between Pakistan and India, with both lobbying the Central Asians for support over the Kashmir issue.

The Saudi Arabians had hoped that the newly independent Turkic states would opt to switch from the Cyrillic to the Arabic script. Officially, Saudi Arabia is heavily involved in Central Asia, supporting the construction of mosques and supplying over one million copies of the Koran. In spite of some reports to the contrary, it appears that the so-called 'Wahhabis' or religious radicals active in the Ferghana Valley have no direct connections with Saudi Arabia. Saudi Arabia, with its different brand of Islam, may be competing against Iran rather than against the secular Turkey. Because of Saudi Arabia's geographical distance and lack of historical, cultural and linguistic ties with Central Asia, Riyadh has been slow to develop economic and political links with the region.

In recent years China has greatly expanded its economic interests in neighbouring Kazakhstan and Kyrgyzstan. Bilateral trade turnover between China and Kazakhstan amounted to $434 million in 1993, almost four times larger than trade turnover between Turkey and Kazakhstan. Over half of Kazakh imports of basic consumer goods originate from China. Commercial ties between China and Kyrgyzstan are evidently more extensive, with China again supplying consumer goods in return for electricity purchases.[82] However, there is less likelihood of competition between Turkey and China than between Turkey and Iran over the construction of new pipelines. Plans to build an oil pipeline from Turkmenistan to Japan via China – the 'project of the century', according to President Niyazov – remain only on paper because of the likely exorbitant costs. In April 1994 Prime Minister Li Peng toured the Central Asian region to boost trade and to secure promises that exiled separatist Turkic groups from China would no longer receive support from Kazakhstan and Kyrgyzstan in particular. There are a number of exiled Uighur groups in Turkey which still advocate the creation of an independent East Turkestan, but these appear to be only a minor irritant in relations between Ankara and Beijing. In reality, Turkey is likely to do little to support Uighur liberation movements. Rather, it would seem that in the near future rivalry may intensify between China and Russia with regard to Kazakhstan, Kyrgyzstan and possibly Tajikistan.

82. Ross H. Munro, 'China's waxing spheres of influence', *Orbis*, vol. 38, no. 4, fall 1994, pp. 600–602.

The leaderships of post-Soviet Central Asia appear to be seeking to develop closer economic and political relations with all interested outside states. Hitherto, it seems that they have still been able to play the field without completely alienating any of the parties seeking to develop closer relations with them. The Central Asians still appear to be in favour of maintaining close economic links with Russia, while at the same time protecting their sovereignty and independence. This will involve a delicate balancing act. In September 1994 Russia succeeded in forming the CIS Interstate Economic Committee, the first executive body of what is meant to be a CIS Economic Union. Turkmenistan opposed the view that this Committee should aim to establish a payments union and refused to attend its first official session in November 1994. Other Central Asian states insisted on the need for consensus to set up a customs union, monetary union or common market.

The formation of a union of economic and defence cooperation between Kazakhstan, Uzbekistan and Kyrgyzstan in the first months of 1994 seems to be part of Nazarbaev's scheme to establish a Euro-Asian Union. There appear to be hopes that this Union, which would include Russia, could somehow lead to close economic interaction between its members without Moscow's domination. At the second Turkic Summit Nazarbaev outlined his scheme for a Euro-Asian Union which would involve the removal of customs barriers and provide for the free movement of peoples and goods among its members. Nazarbaev enthusiastically proposed that this Union could include the CIS and Turkey and possibly even China and Eastern Europe.[83] Within such a grandiose framework this scheme is likely to suffer the same fate as an earlier plan to form an Asian CSCE-type organization – another project of Nazarbaev's which appears to have been aborted or at least temporarily shelved.

83. *TDN*, 20 October 1994.

8 CONCLUSION

A leader article in *The Economist* in September 1991 discussed the possible consequences of the disintegration of the Soviet Union. Noting Turkey's interest in the Black Sea region and its potential to develop ties with the Turkic republics, the article seriously considered the possibility of Turkey becoming a future superpower.[84] It was arguments along these lines that soon gripped the imagination of politicians and public alike in Turkey. Inflated hopes and raised expectations, the products in part of previous ignorance and lack of interest in developments in Central Asia, had to be revised by officials in Ankara after the shortcomings of the first Turkic Summit. While seeking to maintain close links with Turkey, the Central Asians, confronting an acute economic crisis and not prepared to alienate Moscow, were eager to further ties with Russia and other external interested parties.

Although they never espoused the goal of political Pan-Turkism, leading Turkish officials seem to have had to shift their ambitions. The emphasis of the Foreign Ministry at least is now on the need to institutionalize ties between Turkey and the Turkic republics without aiming to establish a form of union or commonwealth. On the other hand, the Turkish Ministries of Education and Culture are not only seeking to reinforce cultural links but, it could be argued, are also engaged in attempting to shape the developing national identities of the Turkic states in Central Asia and the Transcaucasus. The notion of Turkic solidarity remains an important driving force for official circles in Ankara, and also for other agencies, institutes and political parties. Given the current political climate in Turkey, the linkage between a rising 'ethnic' nationalist feeling and the consciousness of a common 'Turkish' identity embracing Turkey and the Turkic states is real. Although the leaderships of the Central Asian 'Turks' themselves do not appear to give equal weight to the importance of Turkic brotherhood, the success of the second Turkic Summit must have been encouraging to officials in Ankara. Furthermore, although Ankara has officially shunned contacts with Pan-Turkic groups in Central Asia, the convening of two meetings of the Turkic Peoples' Assembly in Turkey in the

---

84. *The Economist*, 'Tomorrow's Empires', 21 September 1991, pp. 15–16.

presence of the highest officers of the Turkish state is revealing. The Russian authorities have already perceived such gatherings as signs of emerging Pan-Turkic feeling. Officials in Ankara should remain mindful of such perceptions as they are likely to create problems for Turkish–Russian relations in Central Asia and elsewhere.

Turkish politics are in a state of flux. Between June and December 1994 three Turkish foreign ministers were in office. At the time of writing the position of the current foreign minister, the Social Democrat Murat Karayalçin, is far from secure. Prior to the merger of the Social Democrats and the Republican People's Party in mid-February 1995, there had been much speculation that Çiller would ditch the Social Democrats as her coalition partner and look for support elsewhere. The merger places the immediate future of the Çiller government in doubt, although new coalition parties could still be sought. The National Action Party under Türkeş is already enjoying much closer links with Çiller's True Path Party and supports her tough policy not only against the PKK but also against Kurdish parliamentary deputies accused of having links with the PKK. Nevertheless, for now, and in spite of the increasingly critical line adopted by Mümtaz Soysal in his four months in office as foreign minister, Turkish foreign policy remains firmly pro-Western in its orientation. Increased involvement in Central Asia is not meant to be at the expense of Turkey's development of closer ties with the EU or other groupings.

The leader of the Welfare Party, Necmettin Erbakan, has spoken of his intention to revise Turkish foreign policy should his party form or lead the next government. His new Muslim World Order envisages the formation of an Islamic United Nations, an Islamic NATO, an Islamic Common Market, and an Islamic cultural cooperation organization in which Turkey would play the leading roles. These ideas are bound to alarm Moscow bearing in mind Russia's traditional fears not only of Pan-Turkism but also of Pan-Islam. Iran would also not respond favourably to Erbakan's intention to revive the Caliphate based in Turkey. The Welfare Party has already referred to agricultural cooperation between Turkey, the United States and Israel in Central Asia as part of a 'ten year old Zionist plot'.[85] It is not clear, however, whether the Welfare Party, if it were in power, could reverse the traditional foreign policy of the Turkish Republic, which has been based on developing closer political, economic, social and military links with the West.

The situation in post-Soviet Central Asia is also far from stable. Economic difficulties could lead to renewed civil strife within or even between states in view of the scattered distribution of peoples and other unresolved problems such as the issue of contested boundaries. The troubles in neighbouring Afghanistan and Tajikistan could also spill

85. *TDN*, 3 November 1994.

over and destabilize the region. Here, an Uzbek concern to stem a possible expansion of radical politicized Islam could lead to other Central Asian states – which are traditionally suspicious of Uzbekistan – accusing Uzbekistan of seeking to become a regional hegemon. A change in leadership in Central Asia or in Moscow could also create additional unforeseen problems.

Further instability in the region would pose new challenges to Turkey, Russia and Iran. In such circumstances each state would be more likely to perceive one another as competitors rather than prospective partners. The official line of the Turkish Ministry of Foreign Affairs is to support the policies of all states which are seeking to assist in the democratization of Central Asia.[86] There have been few indicators to date of genuine democratization in the region. The Turkish model of political and economic development has been of little relevance. Turkey, Russia and Iran and other interested states should aim to compete less and cooperate more in developing the Central Asian economies through concerted action in, for instance, improving transportation networks and constructing new oil and gas pipelines. This would contribute greatly towards regional stability and would, in turn, benefit the Central Asians themselves, but it would also be in the interest of all outside concerned parties, including Turkey.

86. Interview with an official in the Turkish Ministry of Foreign Affairs responsible for former Soviet Central Asia, Ankara, 6 December 1994.